Walking Brisbane

BRISBANE

Walking
Brisbane

ALISON COTES AND PAMELA WILSON

First published in Australia in 2000 by
New Holland Publishers (Australia) Pty Ltd
Sydney • Auckland • London • Cape Town

14 Aquatic Drive Frenchs Forest NSW 2086 Australia
218 Lake Road Northcote Auckland New Zealand
24 Nutford Place London W1H 6DQ United Kingdom
80 McKenzie Street Cape Town 8001 South Africa

National Library of Australia
Cataloguing-in-Publication Data:

Cotes, Alison.
Walking Brisbane.
Bibliography.
Includes index.
ISBN 1 86436 511 0
1. Walking – Queensland – Brisbane. 2. Brisbane (Qld) –
Guidebooks. I. Wilson, Pamela II. Title.
919.4310466

Publishing Manager: Anouska Good
Project Editor: Jennifer Lane
Copy editor: Rosanne Fitzgibbon
Designer: Peta Nugent
Layout: David Spratt
Printer: Times Offset, Malaysia

The authors and publishers have made every effort to ensure the information
in this book was correct at the time of going to press and accept no
responsibility for any errors that may have occurred. Prices, opening times,
facilities, locations or amenities can change over time so it is recommended
that the reader call the operator or service and confirm any information that
might be required.

Contents

Acknowledgements | viii • Introduction | 1 • Brisbane's History | 4

Walks in Order of Length | 6 • Key to maps | 7

Walks

Acknowledgements

We would like to express our grateful thanks to the many friendly staff members of the Brisbane, Ipswich and Redcliffe City Councils, and to Greg Hallam of the Cultural Heritage Branch of Queensland's Environment Protection Agency.

Rosanne Fitzgibbon proved yet again to be an unflappable editor, Neil Wiseman lived up to his name, and Patrick Wilson provided much-needed encouragement and support.

Alison Cotes, Pamela Wilson

Introduction

Sprawling, relaxed and friendly, Brisbane is the perfect subtropical city, big enough to offer everything the sophisticated visitor can desire, but small enough to have retained that overgrown country town feeling. The summers may be sticky, but from March to November the weather is perfect, and most Brisbane residents enjoy an outdoor lifestyle that is the envy of their southern neighbours, eating, playing and sometimes even working in the open air.

In his book *Portrait of Brisbane*, Bill Scott describes it as 'a lazy town with its sleeves rolled up, casually sprawling across its thirty-seven hills. The hills are patterned with paling fences, mango trees, high weatherboard houses, and a tangle of overhead wires like the web of a demented spider.'

Brisbane is very different from Australia's other capital cities, as the old joke makes clear. In Melbourne they ask where you went to school, in Sydney how much money you have, in Adelaide where you go to church, and in Perth where you come from. But in Brisbane it is said that they put an arm around your shoulders and ask if you would like a beer.

The city is divided by its great brown river, which is best seen from the air. As you fly in, you can see how the undulating curves bisect the city but then unite it again, the eight major bridges and hundreds of water craft joining the edges as a skilled embroiderer joins two parts of an elaborately patterned patchwork quilt.

The Brisbane River is one of the oldest rivers in the world, they say, formed about 200 million years ago. It is also much longer than most people realise, meandering along for nearly 340 kilometres, and navigable for 88 of them. It houses the third largest seaport in Australia, taking vessels up to 80,000 tonnes, has five weirs, two major tributaries (the Bremer and the Stanley rivers), and a number of creeks of varying size and importance. Upriver near Esk is Lake Wivenhoe, the major dam, two-and-a-half times as big as Sydney Harbour. The river system is a formidable body of water.

In recent years the river has been opened up by the introduction of the City-Cats, sleek catamarans that take passengers up and down the river from Hamilton wharves to The University of Queensland and provide a new way of looking at the city. Many of the walks in this book make use of the CityCats as a fast and exciting way to get started.

Brisbane is a hilly city, nestling in a basin formed by the D'Aguilar Ranges. Away from the flat plains of the river bank the roads wind up and down, meandering along ridges and around corners, lined with bright flowering trees and the darker shades of the great hoop pines, blue gums and Moreton Bay figs. As you wander along these roads you will come across Brisbane's most distinctive architectural feature, the houses known as Queenslanders, unlike anything else in Australia.

Although the first substantial public buildings were made of brick and stone, proclaiming their solid English origin, domestic architecture developed differently. Timber was plentiful and the climate mild, so chamfer boards formed exterior walls and internal walls were made of tongue-and-groove boards.

An old Queenslander, with its corrugated iron roof either creaking in the heat or magnifying the noise of a tropical downpour, and its tongue-and-groove boards moving against each other, seems quite alive in a way that a stone or brick house never can.

Until the late 20th century Brisbane was known as Stump City by its southern neighbours, who still tend to look down their noses at its unique domestic architecture, with most houses raised off the ground on tall wooden stumps capped with metal plates to discourage white ants. But those who live here know that this architectural style allows cool air to circulate, and also provides a space for storage, for drying clothes in the wet season and, most famously of all, for children to play. 'Under the house' has been celebrated by some of Australia's most important writers, especially David Malouf in his 1975 novel *Johnno*.

While children play under the house, their elders congregate on the broad verandahs that often wrap around three sides of the building. In colonial times the inside rooms were only used after dark, when the mosquitoes and midges began to bite, and the verandah is still considered the best room in the house by many people. The custom has been followed even in the modern apartment blocks which now line much of the river bank, and no home unit worthy of the name will be without its balcony or patio. There really is much more to appreciate in Brisbane than its domestic architecture, however. These walks will take you to areas of historical importance, through the lovely parks and gardens for which the city is famous, along the river bank, to charmingly eccentric shopping areas, and to seaside suburbs.

Since the Commonwealth Games were held here in 1982, and especially since World Expo in 1988, Brisbane has developed at a rapid pace, and can no longer be considered the Cinderella city in the north. The Queensland Cultural Centre at South Bank comprises an art gallery, museum, library, and opera and drama theatres with offerings as exciting as anywhere else in Australia, and the vibrant restaurant scene makes the most of the foods found at their best in the tropics – mangoes and other tropical fruit, reef fish and, of course, the famous Queensland mud crab.

The mild winter climate, the wide variety of exotic foods, the brilliance of the flowering trees and, above all, the relaxed friendliness of the people, all helped to earn Brisbane the title of Australia's most livable city. This book will enable you to unlock some of its treasures.

General points

Length: Many of the walks have deliberately been kept short, because in the height of summer the humidity can be oppressive and the hills very tiring. But for those with the stamina, there are suggestions about how to extend some walks, either by taking a different route at the end or by linking it with one of the other walks in the book.

Climate: The climate is hot and humid in the monsoon season (the Wet), which runs from December to March, with the highest rainfall in January and February.

As the average temperature is 30 degrees Celsius, summer days can be oppressive, and from November to February it is probably better to walk early in the morning or late in the afternoon. It is important to take a bottle of water and to wear a hat, as the sun can be fierce, even when it is hidden behind the clouds in the wet season. Although winters are mild, dry and very pleasant, August is the season of notorious cold, dry winds, so it's best to avoid lengthy, unprotected walks. The best months for walking are from April to June and August to October, when the temperature averages around 25 degrees.

Tropical cyclones rarely come as far south as Brisbane, and the dams that have been built on the higher reaches of the river mean it is unlikely that there will be a recurrence of the disastrous floods which devastated the city in 1893 and 1974.

Walking pace: Because of the hills and the heat, it is advisable to take these walks at a leisurely pace. We have assumed an average pace of one kilometre every twenty minutes, but allow longer if you plan to stop for a cold drink or coffee along the way, or deviate from the suggested route.

Brisbane's History

Before white people arrived, the area around the Brisbane River had been occupied for 40,000 years by the people of the Yuggera clan. They spoke one of the group of languages known as Marric, where the word for people is Murri. This word is preferred by the descendants of those first inhabitants, and will therefore be used in this book instead of the whitefella term Aborigine. The first European to chart the Queensland coast was Captain James Cook in 1770, and 19 years later Matthew Flinders explored it more fully, although he missed the mouth of the river.

By the 1820s the administrators of the penal colony at Sydney Cove needed new sites to house 'refractory and incorrigible' prisoners, and so in 1823 Lieutenant John Oxley was sent to explore the northern coast in greater detail. He anchored in what he called Pumice-Stone River, and was met by a group of Murri people, among whom was a white man, Thomas Pamphlett (now commemorated in a bridge across one of the river's tributaries). He and two other escaped convicts, Finnegan and Parsons, had been shipwrecked on Moreton Island and befriended by the Toorbul people. Oxley explored the river for 80 kilometres upstream, and was so impressed by its size and beauty that he named it after Thomas Brisbane, the governor of New South Wales. He did not, however, think it a suitable site for a convict settlement, and recommended that a penal farm be established at Redcliffe.

But when the first commandant Lieutenant Miller was sent there in 1824 with a contingent of convicts and the troops to guard them, he soon realised that Redcliffe was a mistake. The local Murris were not friendly, the coastal mosquitoes were vicious, and there was no permanent fresh water, so a few months later he transferred his unhappy band to the banks of the Brisbane River, at a place called by the Murri people Mi-an-jin.

The third commandant, Captain Patrick Logan, arrived in 1826. He was a harsh brutal man, who soon gained the title of the Tyrant of Brisbane Town. He would commonly order 75 lashes for even a minor misdemeanour, so nobody was surprised or upset when he was murdered while exploring the Brisbane Valley in 1830. As the convict ballad 'Moreton Bay' puts it,

' For three long years I was beastly treated,
And heavy irons on my legs I wore,
My back from flogging was lacerated,
And oft-times painted with crimson gore.
Like the Egyptians and ancient Hebrews
We were oppressed under Logan's yoke,
But a native black there lay in ambush
Did give this tyrant a mortal stroke.'

By 1831 there were 1200 convicts at the settlement, but demand was growing for the fertile area to be opened up to free settlers and in 1842, three years after the penal settlement was disbanded, the ban on free settlers was lifted and the Moreton Bay District began to develop.

When the colony of Queensland was officially separated from New South Wales in 1859, there were 5000 settlers. The 1870s and 1880s were boom times for white immigration. It was during this period that most of the imposing public buildings were constructed, and electric light introduced. The economic depression of the 1890s was made worse in 1893 by two massive floods within weeks of each other, and for two or three decades Brisbane stagnated socially, economically and culturally – in 1906 the Queensland Art Gallery listed only sixty-two 'pictures', and the Brisbane Public Library had fewer books than any other capital city except Hobart.

But sport and live theatre boomed, and racing, cricket and football clubs were established from the very beginning of free settlement, while the city boasted more venues for live drama in the 1890s than it has today.

In 1925, when 24 local authorities joined to form the Brisbane City Council, the city became one of the largest administrative centres in the world. Since then, in spite of governments unsympathetic to the preservation of buildings of cultural importance, enough fine buildings were saved to allow this vibrant young city to retain its solid heritage. From 1982, when the Commonwealth Games were held here, the city has shown itself to be outgoing and culturally innovative, and World Expo in 1988 made it really come alive.

Today, it is the third largest city in Australia after Sydney and Melbourne, with a population of 1.3 million spreading from the shores of Moreton Bay right up the Brisbane River Valley to the foothills of the D'Aguilar Range.

Walks in Order of Length

Some of these walks can be made longer if desired, and the extended length is given in brackets.

New Farm Park | 1.2 km (3 km)

CBD Riverfront | 1.5 km

City Botanic Gardens | 1.5 km

South Bank Parklands | 1.5–2 km

Fortitude Valley | 2 km

Kangaroo Point | 2 km (3.5 km)

Windsor | 2.5–3 km (4.5 km)

The University of Queensland,

St Lucia | 3 km

Boondall Wetlands | 3 km

City Heritage Buildings | 3.5 km

The Valley Art Circuit | 3.5 km

Gregory Terrace | 3.5 km

Spring Hill | 3.5 km (7 km)

Wickham Terrace & City Churches | 4 km

Toowong to the City along the River | 4 km

Mt Coot-tha Botanic Gardens | 4 km

Cleveland | 4 km

Ipswich | 4 km

Redcliffe Peninsula | 4 km (7 km or 9 km)

Brisbane Corso, Highgate Hill

& West End | 4 km (8 km)

Petrie Terrace & Paddington | 4.5 km

Teneriffe & the Old Wharves | 4.5 km

Toowong Cemetery | 4.5 km

Shorncliffe & Sandgate | 4.5 km (5.5 km)

Chelmer | 4.7 km

South Brisbane | 5.5 km (8 km)

Slaughter Falls & Mt Coot-tha | 5.5 km (8 km)

Simpson Falls & the Eugenia Circuit | 6.5 km

Hamilton | 6.5 km (7.5 km)

Wynnum–Manly | 7.5 km (10.5 km)

Key to Maps

 Hospital

 Church

 Parks and gardens

 Information

 Parking

 Bus stop

 Post office

 Gallery

 Public toilets

 Railway station

Route Marks

••◗•••• route of walk

7 key numbers

S walk start

F walk finish

An easy-to-follow illustrative map accompanies each walk. The walk route is clearly marked in green; buildings and sites are dark blue; parks and gardens are green; and 'general' areas are shaded light blue.

On each map the walk route begins at the point **S** and finishes at **F**. Key numbers are located on the map as well as in the walk text. The Key to Maps, left, displays full details of symbols that appear on the maps in order to assist the walker.

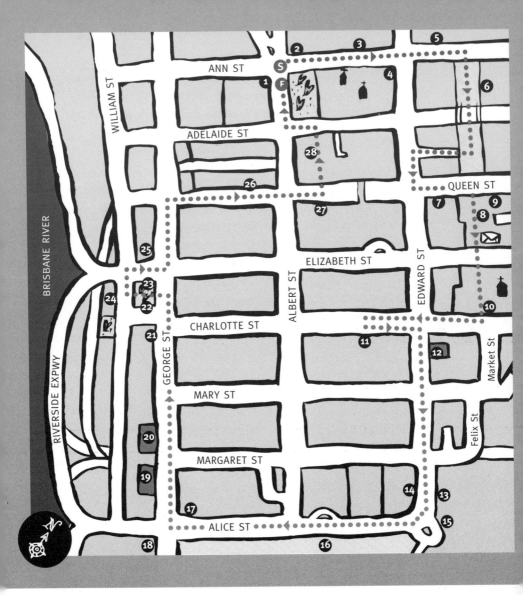

Walk key

1. City Hall | 2. Uniting Church | 3. Brisbane School of Arts | 4. People's Palace | 5. Central Railway Station | 6. Shrine of Remembrance and Anzac Square | 7. MacArthur Chambers | 8. General Post Office | 9. Newspaper House | 10. St Stephen's Cathedral | 11. State Health Building and Charlotte House | 12. Metro Arts Centre | 13. Harbours and Marine | 14. Smellie's Building | 15. Naval Offices | 16. City Botanic Gardens | 17. Queensland Club | 18. Parliament House | 19. The Mansions | 20. Harris Terraces | 21. Sciencentre | 22. Treasury Building (hotel) | 23. Queen's Gardens | 24. Commissariat Stores | 25. Treasury Building (casino) | 26. Queen St Mall | 27. Regent Theatre | 28. Brisbane Arcade

Walk No. 1

City Heritage Buildings
From convicts to commerce

Start/Finish

City Hall, King George Square (corner Adelaide and Albert Streets).

Length/Time

3.5 km/1 hour

Tips

The Brisbane CBD is easy to navigate – streets with women's names run parallel and are crossed by streets with men's names. Streets in the CBD are generally not very steep.

Access

A map of accessible routes for people with disabilities is available free from the Brisbane City Council's Customer Service Centres. The Queen Street Mall has a special Braille Trail made of yellow tiles embedded in the paving. A guide to the trail is also available free from City Council Customer Services Centres.

The City of Brisbane began life in 1825 as the Moreton Bay Penal Settlement, a notorious convict colony for repeat offenders. Nestling inside a bend of the mighty Brisbane River, its incomparable position meant that free settlers soon clamoured to be allowed to take up land in the area, and in 1840 the penal settlement was closed and a prosperous commercial city developed. Although an insensitive government in the 1960s and 1970s, hell-bent on modernising at all costs, bulldozed a number of outstanding colonial buildings, many still remain, combining with the architecture of later periods to create a city both proud of its past and confident of its future. This walk, which roughly follows the route of the Brisbane City Council Heritage Trail, takes in the most important 19th century buildings of the central business district.

Begin the walk at City Hall, fronting King George Square. **City Hall |1|**, a fine sandstone building from the 1920s, houses the council offices but is also an important community centre. A free lift (Mon–Sat 10.30am–4.30pm) takes visitors up to the top of the tower for a great overview of the city.

Noted Brisbane sculptor Daphne Mayo was responsible for the triangular pediment above the entrance celebrating the achievements of the early white settlers, and the historical theme is continued in some of the statuary in King George Square itself, notably the Petrie Tableau, which commemorates the life of an early pioneering family, and Speakers' Corner. Here bronze statues of Emma Miller, revered as the mother of the Labor movement in Queensland, Sir Charles Lilley, an early State premier, and writer Steele Rudd (Arthur Hoey Davis), who created the Dad and Dave characters, make an unlikely trio, while the four modernist bronze sculptures near the fountain have been compared to Daleks from the Dr Who television series.

On the Ann Street side of the square is the **Albert Street Uniting Church |2|**, in Victorian Gothic Revival style. Built in 1889, it is a very popular church for weddings. Walk up Ann Street away from the City Hall, and on the left is the **Brisbane School of Arts |3|**, built in 1865 and, after many disastrous additions, restored to its original glory in 1983.

Across the road is the **People's Palace |4|**, with elaborate cast-iron verandahs. Built in 1911 to provide cheap accommodation for indigent travellers, it is now a popular backpackers' hostel.

Cross Edward Street and notice **Central Railway Station |5|** (1901), with its highly visible clock tower. The Sheraton Hotel is built behind the station, and it is worth stopping for a drink in the lounge to take advantage of the glass-fronted lifts, which provide a splendid view of the city and beyond.

The Shrine of Remembrance

Across Ann Street from the station are the Shrine of Remembrance and **Anzac Square |6|**. Use the pedestrian underpass to gain access to the war memorial rooms (see Opening Times), and to the square itself, a shady grassed area with many monuments to those who served their country during wartime.

From Anzac Square cross Adelaide Street, enter the shopping complex under Post Office Square, and find your way to Rowes Arcade, home to Brisbane's most fashionable café in 1897, and now full of exclusive boutiques. Rowes Arcade comes out in Edward Street. Turn left then left again into Queen Street, and look across to **MacArthur Chambers |7|**. This building, constructed in 1934 and clad in local sandstone, was used by General Douglas MacArthur as his headquarters during the Pacific conflict of the Second World War.

In the same Queen Street block is the **General Post Office |8|**, built by Brisbane pioneer John Petrie in 1871–72. When Brisbane Town was a convict settlement in the 1830s, the Female Factory Prison stood on the site now occupied by the GPO. Philatelists will want to visit the GPO Museum which is housed in this building.

Cheek-by-jowl with the GPO is **Newspaper House |9|**. Like many office buildings of this period, it has been converted into chic inner-city apartments.

St Stephen's Cathedral

Walk through the GPO Arcade, cross Elizabeth Street, and enter the grounds of **St Stephen's Roman Catholic Cathedral |10|**. This imposing porphyry stone building, designed by Benjamin Backhouse in English Gothic style, was begun in 1863, completed in 1874, and has recently been refurbished. The modernised interior is now remarkable for a distinctive baptistery behind the sanctuary, a magnificent rood crucifix, a statue of Mary of Nazareth, and jewel-like Stations of the Cross by noted Australian painter Lawrence Daws.

In the cathedral grounds is the oldest remaining church building in Brisbane, the exquisite Pugin Chapel, designed by the English architect. Now restored as a shrine to Mary McKillop, the interior contains a startling new statue of Australia's first potential candidate for sainthood. Sculptor John Elliott took the trunk of a huge fallen camphor laurel tree, hollowed it out, and sliced it then recombined it so that the figure of Mary McKillop reflects her tough resilience and the rough slab hut in which

Opening Times

City Hall Art Gallery:
daily 10am–5pm daily, except Good Friday, Easter and Christmas
War Memorial Rooms: under Anzac Park: Mon–Fri 9am–2.15pm
Parliament House: telephone 3406 7562 for tour times
Sciencentre: 10am–5pm daily
Old Commissariat Stores: Tue, Wed, Fri 11am–2pm, Thur 10am–4pm

Refreshments

A wide variety of places from atmospheric old pubs to glittering coffee shops.

Route Notes

In 1996 the Brisbane City Council installed a series of bronze plaques in the pavement of Albert Street, featuring quotations about Brisbane from 32 different writers, including famous names like David Malouf, Thea Astley, Steele Rudd and Oodgeroo Noonuccal among other local writers. The plaques are the basis of the Albert Street Literary Trail, chosen for its many bookshops and pavement cafés. A brochure detailing the writers and the position of each plaque is available from the Brisbane City Council's Administration Centre.

she started her first school. Since the statue was unveiled in February 1999 it has attracted both praise and condemnation.

Continue through the cathedral grounds and turn right into Charlotte Street. Cross Edward Street to look at the contrasting architectural styles of the **State Health Building and Charlotte House |11|** (Verlie Just's art gallery in this building has a fine collection of Japanese woodcuts), then return and go right into Edward Street to head towards the City Botanic Gardens.

On the left, between Charlotte and Mary Streets, are the Victory Hotel, a popular watering hole, and the four-storey **Metro Arts Centre |12|**, which houses local arts organisations. Crossing Mary Street, look left for a glimpse of the Story Bridge, Brisbane's most famous landmark.

Commissariat Stores 1829

Near the river

A block further down, across Margaret Street, is one of the finest clusters of Victorian buildings in the city. These include the **Harbours and Marine building |13|**, built by John Petrie in 1878–80, now part of the Heritage Hotel complex. Opposite is the rich red brick façade of **Smellie's Building |14|**, an early warehouse with an unusual baroque doorway in its eastern side.

Next to the Heritage Hotel, fronting the river, are the old **Naval Offices |15|**, one of the few buildings in Brisbane in Queen Anne style. From here turn right into Alice Street with the **City Botanic Gardens |16|** on your left, and walk for two blocks. On the corner of George and Alice Streets is

the huge colonial building housing the exclusive **Queensland Club |17|**, which is not open to the public.

Look diagonally across to **Parliament House |18|**, designed by the official Colonial Architect Charles Tiffin after a nationwide competition. The first meeting of parliament took place in 1868, only three years after the foundation stone was laid. Tours of Parliament House are available (see Opening Times). Turn right into George Street, and pass the softer brick terraces that make up **The Mansions |19|** (1890), and, across Margaret Street the **Harris Terraces |20|** (1867). These fine buildings, less detailed than The Mansions, are the oldest in George Street.

Colonial architecture

The next four blocks of George Street contain some of the best surviving examples of government colonial architecture, most of them classified A by the National Trust. The old Government Printing Office on the left side, between Mary and Charlotte Streets, now contains the **Sciencentre** |21|, a good place to escape the heat and to enjoy the displays and hands-on exhibits (see Opening Times). There is a small admission charge. Just past the Sciencentre is the **Treasury Building |22|**, now the Conrad International Hotel and another classified building. The Gallery Bar of this hotel contains the beautiful 11.5 metre cedar bar from the Polo Club.

Immediately in front of the Conrad Treasury Hotel are **Queen's Gardens |23|**. Notice the statuesque Queen Victoria, now restored to her former glory after years of being incarcerated in a warehouse while the building was converted into a hotel, and former premier T. J. Ryan, whose statue was turned away from the casino while it was being built, so that his good Irish Catholic sensibilities would not be offended. Turn left and walk through Queen's Gardens into William Street where, a little to the left and across the road, you will see the old **Commissariat Stores |24|**, one of the only two surviving convict-built structures in the city centre (see Opening Times).

Come out of the Commissariat Stores and turn left, with the river on your left. Walk past the former State Library building, erected in the late 1870s as a museum, converted into a library in 1900 and now used as storerooms. The bizarre mosaic façade was added to the western end of the building in 1960.

The Mall

Turn right into Elizabeth Street then left into George Street, past the Italianate **Treasury Building |25|** which retains a semblance of elegance despite its refurbishment as a casino. Turn right into the **Queen Street Mall |26|**, now the commercial heart of the city, noting the remaining facades of former buildings – on the corner as you turn into the Mall is the Westpac Bank, erected in 1929, and on the left the old Colonial Mutual Building (1883). Further up on the right are the New York Hotel (1929), Newspaper House (1891), and the Carlton Hotel (1891), all now incorporated into the Myer Centre, Brisbane's main shopping complex.

Continue along the Mall over Albert Street and drop in at the **Regent Theatre |27|**, of which, after a long conservation battle in the 1980s, only the façade and the foyers remain.

Cross the Mall to enter the **Brisbane Arcade |28|**, with its elegant first-floor balconies overlooking an array of boutiques and couturier shops, and walk through to Adelaide Street. Cross the road and walk up the wide steps past the fountain back to King George Square where the walk started.

Walk key

1. Queen's Park gates |
2. Avenue of weeping figs |
3. Iron sculpture by Robert Juniper | 4. Queensland University of Technology |
5. A board giving useful information about the Kangaroo Point cliffs |
6. Rainforest hideaway |
7. Mangrove boardwalk |
8. River Stage | 9. Gardens Café | 10. Old Government House | 11. Walter Hill fountain | 12. Rotunda |
13. Royal Palm Lawn |
14. Lily pond area |
15. Modern stainless steel sculptures |
16. Parliament House |
17. Alice Street gates

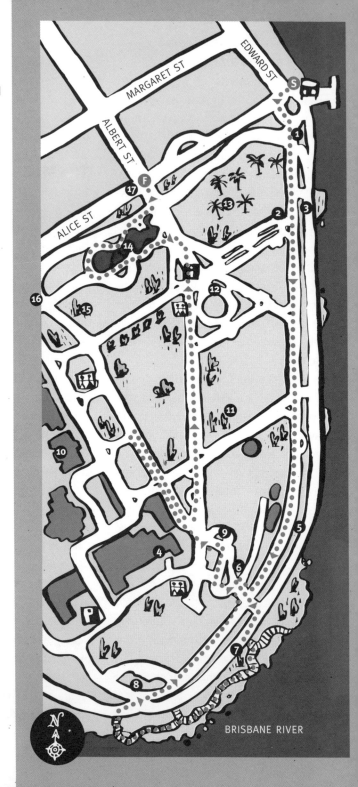

BRISBANE RIVER

City Botanic Gardens

A green oasis in the city

Start

Queen's Park gates, corner of Edward and Alice Streets. Walk to the gates along Edward Street or catch the City Circle bus (333) or the City Sights bus. To reach the gardens by CityCat, get off at the Eagle Street terminal and walk along the boardwalk.

Finish

From either Alice Street main gates or the Queen's Park gates it is an easy walk to the CBD.

Length/Time

1.5–2 km/1 hour. The length of the walk depends upon the number of detours, but allow at least an hour.

Access

Most paths are wheelchair accessible. The Brisbane Mobility Map, available from Brisbane City Council Customer Service Centres, gives details of steps, gradients and accessible toilets and telephones.

Before white settlement, this bend of the river was part of the area known by the local Murri people as Mi-an-jin. In 1828 it was cleared to create farming land for the penal settlement, but in 1855 six acres were added and the area declared a Botanical Reserve. The gardens now cover 20 hectares of land in the centre of the city, with access to the river, Parliament House and Old Government House. The walk, which begins at the massive gates at Edward Street, is ideal on a hot day, and gardeners will be especially interested in the rare and historic plants for which the gardens are famous. Other attractive features of the gardens are a duck pond and a secluded rainforest area.

The walk begins at the impressive **Queen's Park** |1| gates, which were opened in 1865 by the governor Sir George Bowen. Walk along the upper part of the river path. The first road on the right, the Walter Hill Walk, is notable for its **avenue of huge weeping figs** |2|, planted in 1870. An information board close by tells the story of the 1893 floods, including details of a ship that was washed up and stranded in the gardens at the time.

Along the river

At this point look down to the lower river path to a great **iron sculpture by Robert Juniper** |3|, which suggests yacht sails and palm fronds. The lower path provides good views of the Kangaroo Point cliffs.

The small metal structures attached to many of the trees in the gardens provide shelter for the sugar gliders which inhabit the gardens at night. Note also the native Bunya pines, whose nuts were a great delicacy for the local Murri people.

Keep walking along here until you see the buildings of the **Queensland University of Technology** |4| across the park on the right and, a little further along on the left, a small lookout on the river bank, with a board giving useful information about the **Kangaroo Point cliffs** |5|. In the earliest days of white settlement, building stone was quarried from these cliffs. The low buildings along the base of the cliffs are the old Naval Stores, built in 1887.

Turn right into the **rainforest hideaway** |6|, where another plaque quotes renowned novelist Janette Turner Hospital – 'The rainforest smells of seduction, fermentation and death. It smells of Queensland.'

The mangroves

An anticlockwise loop through the rainforest leads back to the main path. Follow the lower path to the **mangrove boardwalk** |7|, which wanders through one of the few remaining stands of the mangroves which originally lined the whole river bank. The massive Brisbane River is still tidal at this point, and at low tide there are stranded jellyfish trapped in the maze of baby mangroves that push their way up through the thick black mud.

Take the boardwalk on the right towards the open river, until it rejoins the main path again, allowing a fine view of the Captain Cook Bridge, named after the great navigator even though he never sailed up this river. A bicycle path which runs five kilometres along the river bank to Toowong begins here (see Walk No. 19), but the gardens walk continues through the metal gates, up a slight slope on the right, and around the back of the River Stage.

Turn left after the yellow boom gates, noticing the **River Stage** |8| as you go, and approach the café either by wandering up the grassy slope or continuing on the paved path above the mangroves. Turn left at the signpost where you began the mangrove walk, and take the path on the left, noting the exotic display of bromeliads and the thick carpet of blue quandong seeds in the summer.

The Café

Take a break in the art nouveau **Gardens Café |9|**, which in less ecologically sensitive times (pre-1958) contained an animal enclosure with monkeys in cages to entertain the public. The walls of the lovely dining room are hung with valuable historical photographs.

From the café, take the left path towards **Old Government House |10|**, now housing the offices of the National Trust. Keep to the upper path, where the steps on the left, sheltered by giant Moreton Bay figs, will bring you to an uninterrupted view of this early Victorian building with its famous kidney-lawn in front.

Retrace your steps and continue straight down the centre path, noticing the **Walter Hill fountain |11|** (1867). The **Rotunda |12|** is situated across the lawns and a path leads to the Alice Street gates. To end the walk at this point, turn right at these gates and wander past the **Royal Palm Lawn |13|** to the Edward Street entrance.

The lily ponds

Alternatively, turn left at the Alice Street gates and wander through the **lily pond area |14|**. Continue clockwise round the pond, the fountain and the waterfall, noticing the **modern stainless steel sculptures |15|** relocated from the World Expo '88 sculpture collection. **Parliament House |16|** is just across the road, but stay in the gardens and turn right until you arrive back at the **Alice Street gates |17|**, from where it is an easy walk into the city.

Opening Times

The gardens are open 24 hours a day, and are well lit at night.

Refreshments

The Gardens Café is situated in a charming Art Nouveau cottage built in 1905, which used to be the house of the curator, a Mr Bailey. Either sit inside in a formal dining room, or indulge in coffee and home-made muffins on a wide sheltered colonial verandah trailing with jasmine.

There are bubbler taps throughout the park, and toilets at the Rotunda, the café, and opposite the Queensland University of Technology.

Route Notes

Bicycles and rollerblades are allowed, and can be hired from 87 Albert Street, about one block up from the gardens. Cyclists must keep to designated pathways and give way to pedestrians, and dogs must be kept on a leash.

Free guided tours run Mon–Sat 11am–1pm, excluding public holidays, leaving from the Information Kiosk just inside the Alice Street entrance. Guided tours including morning or afternoon tea or lunch are also available if booked in advance (3403 8888 Mon–Fri 7am–4pm).

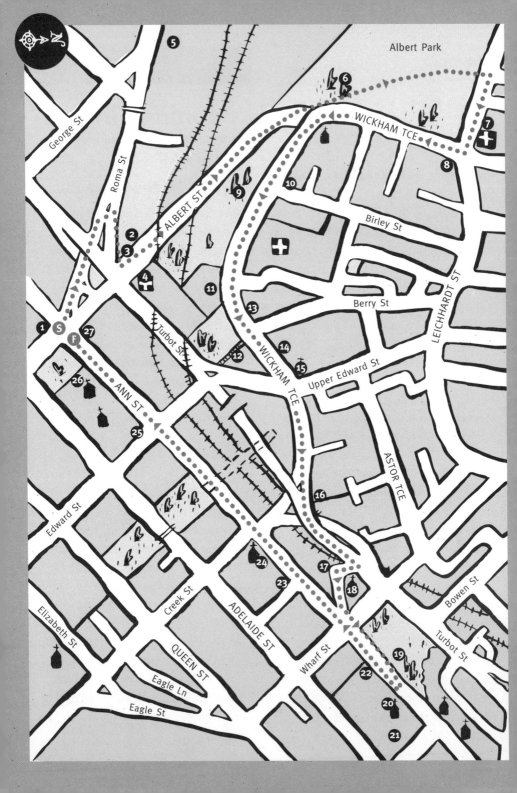

Wickham Terrace & City Churches

The growth of a 19th century city

Start/Finish

The walk begins and ends at City Hall in King George Square.

Length/Time

Just under 4 km/1.3 hours

Access

This is a hilly walk – wear comfortable shoes and a hat, and take some bottled water. Some of the route is accessible by wheelchair – for details check the free Brisbane Mobility Map, available from Brisbane City Council Customer Service Centres.

Free settlers were finally allowed to take up land in 1840, and in the second half of the 19th century the elevated edge of Wickham Terrace was the most fashionable residential street in Brisbane Town. Although the terrace has been taken over by medical offices and boutique hotels, many pleasant buildings still remain, and this walk passes them all, as well as taking in the parks nearby and some of the city's most charming churches. This is the quieter end of the city, with few distractions in the way of shops and restaurants.

Walk key

1. City Hall | 2. Roma Street Forum | 3. Waterfall | 4. Dental School | 5. Transit Centre | 6. Albert Park | 7. St Andrew's War Memorial Hospital | 8. Grand Chancellor Hotel | 9. Wickham Park | 10. Athol Place | 11. The Old Mill | 12. Jacob's Ladder | 13. Craigston | 14. United Services Club | 15. Baptist City Tabernacle | 16. Dods House | 17. All Saints' Anglican Church | 18. St Andrew's Lutheran Church | 19. Cathedral Square | 20. St John's Cathedral | 21. Deanery | 22. St Martin's House | 23. Masonic Temple | 24. St Andrew's Uniting Church | 25. Palace Backpackers' Hostel | 26. Ann Street Presbyterian Church | 27. Albert Street Uniting Church

Begin at **City Hall |1|**, cross Ann Street and follow Roma Street past the Carlton Crest Hotel. At the flyover near the large open-air car park, cross the road into Emma Miller Place, more popularly known as the **Roma Street Forum |2|**. Its official name honours the grand old leader of Labour women in Queensland. This is Brisbane's favourite spot for public meetings and rallies, and stands on the site of the old Brisbane Central Markets.

Walk through the grassed area to the corner of Turbot and Albert Streets, noting the **artificially created waterfall |3|** running over granite boulders as you go. There are seats here, and the sound of the waterfall manages to drown out the roar of the city traffic.

Albert Street

On the corner of Turbot Street, the buff-coloured building on the right is **The University of Queensland's Dental School |4|**. Turn left into Albert Street and walk up the steep hill below the high stone walls of Wickham Park, towering above the city.

The lamps in this street are particularly attractive, and the park itself boasts some large old trees. On the way up Albert Street, look left down to the city's main traffic terminal, where the black glass tower of the **Transit Centre |5|** makes a striking contrast to the more elegant platforms of Roma Street Railway Station, the interstate train terminus.

Beyond the railway station lie the old marshalling yards, now something of an eyesore, though the current feeling is that the site should be transformed into parkland. At the top of the hill on the left, dominated by a large modern sculpture, is **Albert Park |6|**, a good place to rest for a while. Walk up through Albert Park, keeping Wickham Terrace on your right, until you notice **St Andrew's War Memorial Hospital |7|** across the road.

At this point cross over to the **Grand Chancellor Hotel |8|** and go back down the Wickham Terrace hill (noting the pleasingly restored old Queenslander occupied by the Brisbane Theosophical Society at No. 355) until you come back to the intersection with Albert Street.

Follow Wickham Terrace as it turns left. Across the street is **Wickham Park |9|**, which you earlier saw from below, a large green space of shady trees and extensive views of the western part of the city. Around 7am, the van of the Ecumenical Coffee Brigade, one of Brisbane's most enduring charitable ventures, dispenses free coffee and sandwiches here to the local rough diamonds, who either sleep out in the park or live in the cheap boarding houses around this area. They are a cheerful bunch who are always willing to give you the time of day.

Wickham Terrace

Keep walking down the left side of Wickham Terrace, where two original houses still stand – the iron lace and lattice work of **Athol Place |10|** are particularly beautiful, while No. 287, a little further downhill, is much grander, and can only be glimpsed through the front fence.

Pass the Holy Spirit Hospital, and as the street curves to the left, cross the road to Brisbane's oldest remaining building, the Observatory, or the **Old Mill |11|**. Built by convict labour in 1829 at the command of the infamous Captain Logan (whose mysterious murder, either by convicts or local Murri people, was regretted by nobody), its treadmill was the most dreaded punishment in the colony after the lash.

At least one public hanging took place here, but after free settlement it was used for more acceptable purposes, as a signal station for shipping, for television broadcasting experiments in the 1930s, and as a lookout tower by the Fire Brigade. In 1922 the site was declared a park, and today its tranquil appearance gives no indication of its murky past.

Next to the Observatory is another park, named in honour of King Edward VII, where a steep flight of steps – for obvious reasons known as **Jacob's Ladder |12|** – descends into Upper Edward Street. These are more pleasant to look at than they are to navigate.

The left side of Wickham Terrace is dominated by medical specialist consulting rooms, but some original buildings remain – No. 217, **Craigston |13|**, was once a smart residential property, and further towards Edward Street is the **United Services Club |14|**, one of the most beautiful buildings in the city. Built between 1906 and 1908 as a private hotel, it is now open only to members.

Opening Times

The only buildings open to the public along this route are the churches themselves, although some are kept locked during the day for fear of vandalism. It is often possible to ring the administrators of the individual places of worship to have the buildings opened – telephone numbers are displayed on noticeboards.

Refreshments

There are cafés at the top of Albert Street, and the Grand Chancellor Hotel has quiet lounges for a cold drink after the walk up the Albert Street hill.

Route Notes

There are public toilets in City Hall, the Roma Street Forum and in city hotels.

City churches

Next door, on the corner of Upper Edward Street, is the **Baptist City Tabernacle |15|**, rather forbidding from the outside, but remarkable inside for the beauty of its pews and the glory of its geometrically patterned stained glass windows. Between 9am and 2pm there is usually someone there to admit visitors, but telephone beforehand (3831 1613) to make sure.

Cross Upper Edward Street and keep walking down the left side of Wickham Terrace. The right side is dominated by a stark but architecturally significant car park, designed by award-winning Brisbane architect James Birrell in 1959.

Doctors' consulting rooms have spoiled this part of the terrace, but **Dods House |16|**, one of the few original buildings in the block, now calls itself 'the ultimate gentleman's restaurant'. Inchcolm, another old-timer, has just been converted from doctors' rooms to an apartment building.

At the junction of Turbot Street and Wickham Terrace, cross the road carefully (traffic is very busy here) into the grounds of **All Saints' Anglican Church |17|**, one of the oldest churches in the city centre and the second to occupy this site. Designed by architect Robert Suter in local pink porphyry stone and dedicated in 1869, the Gothic-style church has an important hammer-beam ceiling and some very beautiful stained glass. It is usually kept closed, but if you inquire at the hall directly below the church it is sometimes possible to gain admittance.

The much more modern **St Andrew's Lutheran Church |18|** stands across the road from All Saints, its sweeping brick roof suggesting the universal Christian symbol of a boat. From here, with St Andrew's and All Saints behind you, cross Wharf Street into **Cathedral Square |19|**, with its modern landscaping, pretty flower beds, and huge sun sails.

Walk through the square and cross Ann Street to **St John's Anglican Cathedral |20|**,

The Old Mill

one of the finest examples of Gothic revival architecture in the southern hemisphere. The exterior is of Brisbane porphyry and the interior of Helidon sandstone, and cathedral guides are on duty Mon–Fri 10am–4pm, and Saturday and Sunday 10am–12.30pm, to show visitors around the interior.

The foundation stone was laid in 1901, but building did not begin until 1906 because of a shortage of funds. It is still not finished, but if the current building project goes to schedule, the building will be completed by the time of its centenary, and will at last fulfil the vision of its original architect.

Behind the cathedral is the impressive **Deanery |21|**, the oldest building in this area. Built in the 1850s as a private residence, it was known as Adelaide House because of its frontage to Adelaide Street, and the proclamation which created the Colony of Queensland was read from its balcony in December 1859. Since 1899, when it was bought by the Church of England, it has been occupied by the Dean of the cathedral, and is not open to the public.

In the cathedral grounds stands the architecturally eclectic **St Martin's House |22|**, built in 1922 to harmonise with other buildings in the cathedral precinct. Formerly a hospital but now housing the diocesan offices, it is not open to the public.

On the corner of Ann and Wharf Streets is the Brisbane Tavern, once a gracious colonial building with open verandahs and an impressive collection of hanging pot plants, but now a sad reminder of the atrocities perpetrated by over-zealous restoration. Look across Ann Street for another view of All Saints Church where, in an open-air meditation centre, there is a statue by Andor Meszaros of Christ accepting the cross.

Down Ann Street

Keep walking down Ann Street and across Hutton Lane where the old **Masonic Temple |23|** stands proud and unaltered, and men in evening dress with mysterious suitcases still attend regular meetings. The Rothbury building next door, like many Victorian edifices, has been converted into apartments, but one side benefit of modernisation is NPZ Elliot's, an excellent bar and brasserie on the ground floor.

On the corner of Creek Street is the red brick fortress of **St Andrew's Uniting Church |24|**, its grim exterior belied by the softer beauty of the interior with rows of polished wood pews. It is usually open Mon–Fri 9am–4pm (3221 2400).

The final part of this walk is also included in the inner-city heritage walk (Walk No. 1), passing Central Railway Station with the Sheraton Hotel towering above it, Anzac Square, and the **Palace Backpackers' Hostel |25|**. When this was the Salvation Army's People's Palace no alcohol was allowed on the premises, so the backpackers in the cellar bar would appreciate that some things have definitely changed for the better.

Down from the Palace is the tiny white **Ann Street Presbyterian Church |26|**, its severe simplicity making a strong contrast with its neighbour across the road, the **Albert Street Uniting Church |27|**, built in 1889 in the striking Victorian Gothic revival style. Its dark brick elaborately picked out with pale New Zealand limestone makes it the centre of attention, almost outshining the City Hall, where this walk ends.

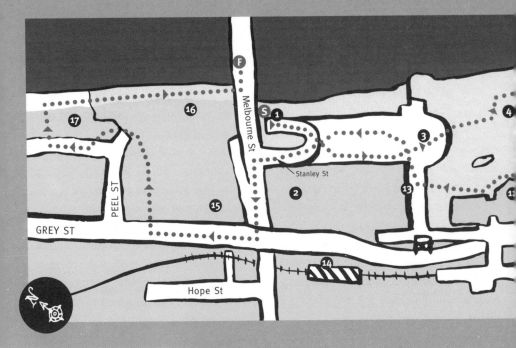

Walk key

1. Stone arch | 2. Performing Arts Complex | 3. Flag Court | 4. Nepalese temple | 5. CityCat Pontoon | 6. City Beach | 7. Boardwalk | 8. Maritime Museum | 9. Grand Arbour | 10. Stanley Street Plaza | 11. Suncorp Piazza | 12. Conservatorium of Music | 13. Playhouse Theatre | 14. South Brisbane Railway Station | 15. Queensland Museum | 16. Queensland Art Gallery | 17. State Library

Start/Finish

At the Performing Arts Complex in Melbourne Street. Take City Bus 300, 301, 306, 322 from the corner of Adelaide and Edward Streets. Train to South Brisbane Railway Station from Roma Street and Central or CityCat across the river from North Quay (disabled access both sides).

Length/Time

1.5–2 km/1 hour. This walk can be as long or as short as you like, but allow at least an hour. It is possible to spend a whole day here without getting bored.

Access

Hats, sturdy shoes and, if it's a hot day, swimsuits – City Beach may be artificially created, but with its white sands and filtered saltwater it is as good as the genuine article. There are changing rooms, lockers and even a lifeguard. Most areas have ramps for wheelchair access.

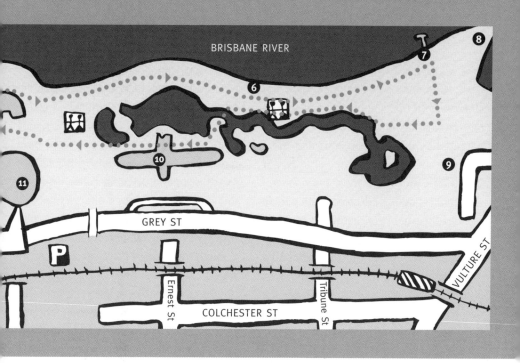

BRISBANE RIVER

GREY ST

P

Ernest St

COLCHESTER ST

Tribune St

VULTURE ST

Walk No. 4

South Bank Parklands
The people's playground

Created on the site of World Expo '88, a seminal six-month event that marked a watershed in Brisbane's cultural coming-of-age, the South Bank Parklands have proved to be just as much of a drawcard. With easy access by ferry, train and bus, and with its vast and varied spaces, the Parklands offer a wide variety of things to do and sights to see, most of them free.

This walk is only a guide to ensure that you don't miss some of the less obvious delights of this eclectic playground. For those with more serious cultural interests, there are suggestions for exploring the Queensland Cultural Centre, which consists of the Performing Arts Complex, Museum, Art Gallery and State Library.

Begin the walk at the river end of the Performing Arts Complex, near the **stone arch** |1| that stands as a reminder of the old Victoria Bridge that was severely damaged by the floods of 1893 and 1896. The arch also commemorates little Hector Vasili, who was killed by a truck loaded with soldiers during the celebration parade marking the end of the First World War.

With the river on the left, walk down the paved area by the side of the **Performing Arts Complex** |2|, with its stepped walls and huge plate glass windows. This is the second stage of the Queensland Cultural Centre, the work of local architect Robin Gibson. The first section, containing the 2000-seat Lyric Theatre, the 1500-seat Concert Hall and the smaller Cremorne Theatre, was opened in 1985, while at the eastern end is the latest addition, the 850-seat high-tech Playhouse Theatre.

The **Flag Court** |3|, its graded steps and cascading fountains almost irresistible to small children, is straight ahead. Turn left here and walk a few metres to the exquisite carvings of the **Nepalese temple** |4|, more correctly but less usually known by its real name, the Nyatpola Pagoda. This is one of the few buildings remaining from World Expo '88 and its plaque, which reads 'May peace prevail on earth', is echoed by the tranquillity of the building itself.

River and rainforest

This part of the parklands is covered with cool rainforest, and it's fun to wander along the boardwalks and get lost in the nooks and crannies. Eventually, however, return to the river path, downriver from the **CityCat pontoon** |5|. Continue walking downriver, keeping in front of the big blue block of buildings where the cafés have one of the best views in Brisbane. Café San Marco is a good place for coffee or a cold drink, and at weekends it offers a front-row view of the many wandering street performers who provide free entertainment all through the day – stilt walkers, mime artists, musicians and circus performers are just some of the artists you may see. The river path is always busy, and this area is a paradise for people-watchers, where cyclists and the cheerful young on rollerblades happily make way for families with grandparents and babies in prams.

There is a children's playground and a free barbecue area just past the restaurant block and then, surrounded by pandanus palms, is everybody's favourite, **City Beach** |6|, a Mecca for toddlers and adults alike. On one side of the wooden bridge that meanders over the water is a shallow paddling area, while the deeper water on the other side attracts older swimmers. There is usually a lifesaver on duty, complete with familiar red and yellow cap.

From here, wander wherever your fancy takes you, but don't forget to walk down to the very end of the river path, where there is another cluster of coffee shops and eating places on the **boardwalk** |7| which juts out over the river. This area is less crowded than the Victoria Bridge end, and provides the best views of the mangrove flats below Parliament House, the Queensland University of Technology across the river and the Captain Cook Bridge which sweeps across to the Riverside Expressway.

People with the smell of the sea in their nostrils may like to leave the parklands at the end of the boardwalk and wander along the pedestrian path to the old **Maritime Museum |8|** (see also Walk No. 8). The *Diamantina* on her own is worth a visit, but the superb dry dock she sits in (1880) is a magnificent example of 19th century craftsmanship, as beautifully built as an ancient Greek theatre.

The museum itself has interesting historical displays, and is especially informative about current salvage operations from early shipwrecks along the treacherous north coast of the Great Barrier Reef. The steamship *Forceful*, now used as a pleasure craft, takes people on picnics to the offshore islands and, on Good Friday each year, to the mouth of the river to see the start of the Brisbane to Gladstone yacht race.

Green grandeur

Walk away from the river now, past the Park Avenue Apartments to the fountains and walkways that distinguish this part of the parklands. The **Grand Arbour |9|**, constructed during 1999, is a giant winding pathway framed by 411 curving columns supporting the vibrant flowers of the Bougainvillea Magnifica. This impressive project, completed early in the year 2000, is part of the South Bank Masterplan. The way back to the Performing Arts Complex

Opening Times

South Bank Parklands: open 24 hours a day, and well patrolled at night.
Performing Arts Complex: guided tours Mon–Fri 12 noon from the main foyer.
Queensland Art Gallery: daily 10am–5pm.
State Library: daily 10am–5pm.
Queensland Museum: daily 10am–5pm.
IMAX Theatre: daily sessions 10am–10pm (3844 4222 for program details).

Refreshments

Everything from restaurants to coffee shops, from takeaway food stalls to ice-cream barrows. Closing times vary according to the time of year and customer demand.

Route Notes

At weekends, there is plenty of free entertainment on the boardwalk and pathways, as well as ticketed shows in the Suncorp Stadium and the new IMAX Theatre. The South Bank Crafts Village Markets take over in the Stanley Street Plaza Fri 5pm–10pm, Sat 11am–5pm, Sun 9am–5pm. Telephone the Visitor Information Centre 8am–6pm (3867 2051), or the 24-hour Entertainment Infoline for recorded information (3867 2020).

leads past more restaurants (try Captain Schnapper for takeaway fish and chips), and eventually to the **Stanley Street Plaza |10|**.

This is the place to down a XXXX (Queensland's local beer) on the verandah of the Plough Inn, the original pub on this site; to shop until you drop at Opal World; destroy your tooth enamel at the Great Aussie Sweet Shop; learn how to snorkel at the South Bank Dive and Hire shop; enjoy a magical moment in the Butterfly House, which has Australia's largest collection of live butterflies (entry fee); or hire a golf buggy, a wheelchair or a stroller. The Visitors' Information Centre has free maps and information brochures, and markets are held here on Friday, Saturday and Sunday.

Across the underground carpark and Grey Street is the IMAX Theatre, which has regular sessions every day (see Opening Times). Keeping to the parklands, however, continue past the huge open-plan **Suncorp Piazza |11|**, the venue for major concerts and cultural events, details of which are posted on boards outside.

The path runs past the **Conservatorium of Music |12|**, built to suggest a treble clef, and ends in front of the **Playhouse Theatre |13|** in the Performing Arts Complex.

To finish the walk at this point, return along the side of the Performing Arts Complex and take the bus, train or ferry.

The Cultural Centre

To continue a little longer, go to the front of the Performing Arts Complex and notice the shell fountain and the outdoor café

South Bank Parklands

tables under great white sun sails. The PAC itself is not always open to casual visitors, but there are guided tours Monday to Friday from the main foyer (see Opening Times), and the Ticket Sales foyer is always open. Walk up the steps and cross Melbourne Street via the flyover, stopping halfway across to look to your right at the city centre across the river, and left to **South Brisbane Railway Station |14|**, built in 1891, with sloping corrugated street awnings supported by cast-iron Corinthian columns and large brackets.

Across Melbourne Street are the other sections of the Queensland Cultural Centre. To the left is the **Queensland Museum |15|** (see Opening Times), where there are usually fascinating special exhibits as well as everybody's favourite, the singing whales suspended above the entrance foyer. After a visit to the Museum, follow the signs to the **Queensland Art Gallery** |16| and the **State Library** |17|, all designed by Robin Gibson, their massive grey forms creating a sense of integrated solidity and beauty.

The interior of the Art Gallery is notable for its water malls and open spaces, and there is a pretty café with an outdoor eating area close to a still pool and some fine outdoor sculptures. From here, walk across to the State Library (see Opening Times), which like the Art Gallery has a very tempting gift shop, and then wander down to the river bank and return along the boardwalk to Victoria Bridge and Melbourne Street. This ends the extended walk.

Walk key

1. Centenary Place | 2. All Hallows |
3. St Ann's House | 4. Cathedral Place |
5. Chinatown | 6. Chinatown Mall |
7. Burlington Asian Supermarket | 8. Story
Bridge | 9. Empire Hotel | 10. Brunswick Street
Mall | 11. McWhirters | 12. Prince Consort Hotel |
13. Presbyterian Church | 14. Sabbath School |
15. Fortitude Valley Post Office | 16. Wickham
Hotel | 17. Valley Baths | 18. Holy Trinity
Anglican Church

Start

Wickham Street at Centenary
Place. City Bus 470, 334, 190, 191,
475, 476 from Elizabeth Street,
or City Bus 300, 370, 375, 379,
380, 381 from Adelaide Street.

Finish

Corner of Ann and James Streets.
All City Buses from here go
back to the city.

Length/Time

2 km/0.75 hours

Access

This is a relatively easy walk,
with plenty of shelter and seats
to rest on. There are no major
hills and most of the walk is
suitable for wheelchairs.

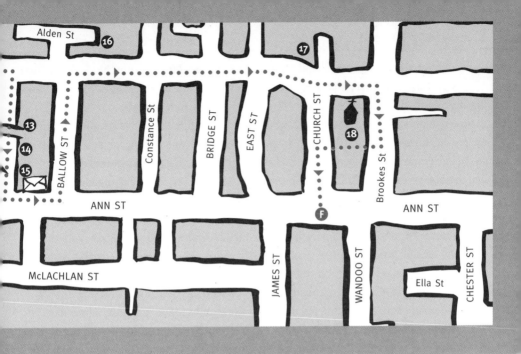

Alden St 16
17
Constance St
BRIDGE ST
EAST ST
CHURCH ST
18
Brookes St
13
14
15
BALLOW ST
ANN ST
F
ANN ST
McLACHLAN ST
JAMES ST
WANDOO ST
Ella St
CHESTER ST

Walk No. 5

Fortitude Valley
Cosmopolitan eccentricity

Every big city has its special area of seedy glamour, and Brisbane's Fortitude
Valley is the equivalent of London's Soho or Sydney's Kings Cross. The inner
city suburb is named after the ship which brought some of the first free
settlers to Moreton Bay when the penal colony was opened up in 1849.
Presbyterian minister John Dunmore Lang and 256 free immigrants settled
in the swampy area just north of Brisbane, but they would be turning in
their graves if they knew how their respectable little district changed over
the course of 150 years, becoming an important commercial centre in the
1880s and 1890s, but going downhill rapidly after that. This walk passes
most of the remaining 19th century buildings, including some beautiful
old pubs, and takes in Chinatown as well.

Get off the bus in Wickham Street opposite **Centenary Place** |1|, once the home of soapbox orators but now occupied almost solely by pigeons, who delight in decorating the statues of Irishman T. J. Byrnes, premier of Queensland just before Federation, and the Scottish poet Robert Burns. Opposite is **All Hallows School** |2|, where the white iron lace of **St Ann's House** |3| presents a serene face to the traffic roaring frantically past.

Walk up Wickham Street on the left, noticing **Cathedral Place** |4|, a commercial and residential complex constructed on the site once proposed for the Roman Catholic Holy Name Cathedral. The prevailing myth is that the funds mysteriously disappeared when some not-so-reverend gentleman took the money to Rome to be blessed by the pope, then absconded with it, but the truth is that after the Second World War the diocese decided to spend its money on schools and nursing homes.

Between Gotha and Gipps Streets is a cluster of outdoor adventure shops, but their equipment will not be needed for this walk, except perhaps a hat if you have forgotten to bring one, or a water bottle.

Chinatown

After Gipps Street cross to the right side of Wickham Street, to the beginning of **Chinatown** |5|, crammed with restaurants and specialty food stores. The Chinese cake shop usually has extraordinary displays in the window, but the best shops are in the **Chinatown Mall** |6|, one block down. Turn right into the Mall past the two huge stone dragons which guard it.

Most of the buildings here date from the beginning of the century, and the painted facades of their upper storeys make an odd contrast with the elaborately decorated Chinese pagodas and walkways at ground level. The **Burlington Asian Supermarket** |7| is worth a visit, before you rest to examine your purchases under the carved painted ceilings of one of the pagodas. Chinatown comes alive during the Asian New Year with parades, fireworks and dragon dances, but this is only one of many festivals that take place here – telephone the Valley Business Association on 3252 5999 for current information.

Continue through the Mall, past the waterfall and through the decorative arch to Ann Street. Look back for a view of the **Story Bridge** |8|, regarded by many as the city's most distinctive architectural symbol, and the high stone convict-built wall below All Hallows School.

Heading down Ann Street away from the city, before you turn left into the Brunswick Street Mall, look across the road at the **Empire Hotel** |9|, one of four major hotels built during the boom period of the 1880s. Its Italianate balconies and balustrades are extraordinarily ornate, although they pale into insignificance when compared with the interior of the Press Club, one of the hotel's liveliest bars, at the end of the Brunswick Street frontage.

Murris in the Mall

The **Brunswick Street Mall** |10| is shaded by tall leopard trees and potted palms and thronged with pavement cafés and, on Saturday from 7am–4pm, eccentric market stalls. The Valley's population encompasses all kinds of people, and time spent sipping a coffee in the Mall is never wasted, with the passing parade of the best and worst of humanity always intriguing and delighting.

There is a strong Murri presence in the Valley, celebrated in the Mall by a huge mosaic of the Rainbow Serpent set into the pavement, and a mural depicting the mythical Dreaming, the time before human beings came into existence.

The upper façades of the commercial buildings in the Mall are architecturally outstanding: on the left, towards Wickham Street, are Ruddle's Buildings (1901), with a unique set of pediments; the T. C. Beirne store (1902), once a major retail store rivalling those in the city centre; and, on the corner of Wickham Street, the Swift and Grice building (1903), originally a jewellery store and one of the most elaborately decorated buildings in the Valley. Notice the corrugated iron mansard roof and turrets, and the many domes and arches. This area used to be known as The Valley Corner. Across the Mall from Swift and Grice's is an equally impressive building, **McWhirters** |11|, which also used to be a huge department store. The first section, five storeys in red brick, was built in 1912, a four-storey addition in Brunswick Street

Opening Times

Most shops in the Valley are open Mon–Fri 9am–5pm, Sat 9am–4pm.

Refreshments

Plenty of cafés and restaurants – try the Press Bar in the Empire Hotel for its bizarre décor, the California Café on the corner of Brunswick and McLachlan Streets for a genuine 1950s feel, and any of the pavement cafés in the Brunswick Street Mall. The Continental is the oldest café in this part of Brisbane.

Route Notes

Many of the heritage buildings listed are privately owned and not open for public inspection – check before entering any building.

followed in 1923, and in 1930 the art deco corner façade was added. The building ceased trading as a department store in the 1980s, and has since been converted into market-type stalls and retail outlets.

As you leave the Mall to turn right into Wickham Street, look back towards the city at the wonderful cast-iron verandahs of the **Prince Consort Hotel |12|** (1888), each with a different pattern. At the end of McWhirter's Wickham Street wall, a plaque has been erected by the Queensland Women's Historical Society telling the story of white settlement in the area.

Nightclubs, pubs and other pleasures of the flesh

Turn right into Warner Street. Halfway along, on the opposite side, is the huge **Presbyterian Church |13|**, built in 1885 to hold 1500 worshippers, most of them families of the free settlers who arrived in the Valley in the ship *The Fortitude* in 1849. They would be horrified to know that their place of worship, and the small adjoining **Sabbath School |14|**, have become trendy nightclubs. Those interested in unconventional shopping should take a detour by turning right into Ann Street at this point, where a Murri art gallery and a plethora of second-hand clothing shops rub shoulders with some of the Valley's more bizarre establishments, including the Red Garter nightclub and Lucky's Trattoria, famous for its green gnocchi for at least forty years.

Otherwise turn left and continue down Ann Street, crossing Ballow Street to look

McWhirters Building

back at the gracious **Fortitude Valley Post Office |15|**, heritage listed but now sadly in a state of disrepair. Built in 1887 to a design by the Colonial Architect, it is one of the most sumptuous buildings in Brisbane, with decorative mouldings and masonry.

Continue walking along Ballow Street until you reach Wickham Street, where across the road is the **Wickham Hotel |16|** (1855), with cantilevered verandahs and a curved corrugated iron roof. The Wickham is famous for two things – the excellent Grape bottle shop, and the swinging gay bar downstairs.

Walk quickly along the next three blocks, for there is very little shade and nothing to see. But on the left, opposite East Street, are the **Valley Baths |17|**, whose red brick and cream render façade suggest 1930s retro gone mad, but is in fact original, retained by an imaginative City Council during the $2 million development of the complex in 1985.

The architectural style of the façade is echoed in the Fortitude Valley Police Station, on the corner of Brookes Street. Built in 1936, it is typical of but grander than other police stations of this period. Cross Wickham Street and walk down the left side of Brookes Street, where a fine old Methodist church, built in 1888 in Gothic revival style, is living out its days as the headquarters of a building cladding company, after a brief period in the 1980s as an alternative theatre.

A gracious church

On the other side of the street **Holy Trinity Anglican Church |18|** has fared much better, still functioning as the centre of a parish with a lively ministry. Walk through the grounds to see the rectory on the left and the church on the right. The rectory, although shabby, is a fine example of late 19th century clergy housing, and its iron lace verandahs are particularly attractive.

In the grounds there is a flat sculpture in the form of an effigy. Called Perigrinata, it was installed in 1998 and, according to the rector, represents 'man, who has come forth from the soil and is returning to the soil, fortified by his faith'.

The church itself, built in 1877, is usually left open, and provides a cool welcome sanctuary on a hot day. The interior seems much more roomy than it actually is, because of the open structure of cast-iron columns and arches. A free pamphlet inside the church gives a detailed architectural history.

Outside, notice the church hall, built in 1891 in red brick, an unusual building material for the period. With the church and the rectory it forms part of an important urban landscape, where mature trees and grassed areas create an island of calm between two busy arterial roads.

The main west door of the church faces Church Street, where a group of modern town houses blend sensitively with more sober 19th century buildings. Turn left into this street and make your way to Ann Street, where a number of different buses go back to the inner city.

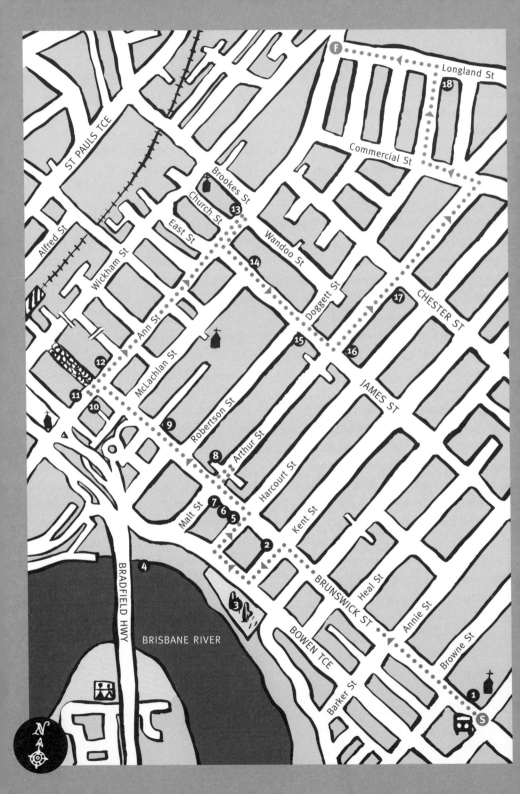

The Valley Art Circuit
A cultural trek

Start

Brunswick Street, New Farm.
City Bus 190, 191 from Adelaide
and George Streets and
to stop 10.

Finish

Corner of Ann and Longland
Streets, Newstead. City Bus 470.

Length/Time

3.5 km/1.5 hours, plus the time
spent in galleries and shops.

Access

Avoid stretches of commercial
development by hopping on a
bus for a few blocks. Wear very
comfortable walking shoes and
take a hat. Most galleries do
not have wheelchair access.

One of Brisbane's happiest innovations is called The Art Circuit, a tour of the city's most exciting and distinctive arts precinct. A green Hail and Ride bus covers the area every 15 minutes, but a walk along the same route provides a better opportunity to appreciate the wide range of fine arts, Murri art, sculpture, craft and installations in the seventeen galleries participating in the project. This area is peppered with cafés, pubs, restaurants and off-beat shops, and includes pockets of residential interest. If the art galleries are your sole reason for taking this walk, ensure that you begin after midday, and avoid Sunday and Monday, when most galleries are closed.

Walk key

1. Wynberg | 2. Brunswick Hotel | 3. Wilson Outlook Reserve | 4. Story Bridge | 5. La Scala | 6. Murri mural | 7. Fusions Gallery | 8. Philip Bacon Gallery | 9. The old Empire Office Building | 10. Empire Hotel | 11. Institute of Modern Art | 12. Fire-Works Gallery | 13. Celestial Glass Studio | 14. Merlo's coffee factory | 15. Bellas | 16. Queen's Arms Hotel | 17. One of the earliest houses in the district | 18. Doggett Street Studio

The walk begins at bus stop 10 in Brunswick Street. Turn back from the bus stop towards the city, and very soon you will pass **Wynberg** |1| at No. 790, with an iron fence on stone foundations, and a heavy iron gate between carved stone gateposts. The house, slightly altered since it was built in 1880, still retains its low elegant lines and steep gabled roof with a dormer window, and is sheltered by a well-developed garden with a fountain. Since the mid-1920s the house has been the official residence of the Roman Catholic archbishop of Brisbane.

Just past Wynberg, on the right, is a small precinct of galleries, bookshops, cafés and excellent restaurants, and it's worth spending a few minutes exploring some of them.

Views of the river

Three blocks along on the left from Barker Street, at the corner of Kent Street, is the **Brunswick Hotel** |2|, which dates from the boom period of the 1880s. Walk left and along Kent Street until you come to the **Wilson Outlook Reserve** |3|, on the other side of Bowen Terrace, with superb views of the river and the **Story Bridge** |4|. Bowen Terrace is one-way at this point, but walkers can proceed against the flow of the traffic to turn right into Harcourt Street. At the corner of Brunswick Street is the grand Federation mansion now called **La Scala** |5|, a three-storey timber-framed structure listed by the National Trust of Queensland now used as a private residence and professional offices.

Adjoining La Scala are several large houses built on top of a three-metre cliff, including a lofty art deco construction in cream stucco. Along the base of the cliff is a brightly painted **Murri mural** |6| with a brass plaque which reads 'Elley Bennett, bantam weight and feather weight champion 1948–1954. Australian Boxing Legend'.

The gallery trek

The next cross street is Malt Street, where an old Methodist church, built in 1876 in the Gothic style, now houses **Fusions Gallery** |7|, which specialises in hand-blown glass and cheerful ceramics. Across Brunswick Street, in an unobtrusive two-storey building in Arthur Street, is the **Philip Bacon Gallery** |8|, perhaps the city's most prestigious, run by Brisbane identity Philip Bacon, whose artists include Sidney Nolan, Robert Dickerson, Margaret Olley, Lawrence Daws, Fred Williams, Charles Blackman and Arthur Boyd.

Turning back into Brunswick Street, and walking now on the right side of the road, you will find a cluster of small galleries with everything from hand-made furniture to eccentric gifts and paintings.

If the day is hot, an ice-cream stop at the Gelateria Venezia in the Central Brunswick precinct, just across the road before Ivory Street, provides a welcome break, with ice-cream which even Italians admit is as good as you'll get outside Italy. The Central Brunswick precinct, with its shops, restaurants and residential apartments, is typical of the intensive restoration that is going on in this part of the city, transforming it from a seedy area where it used to be unsafe to walk at night into an exciting centre for modern living.

A little further down, on the other side of the street on the corner of Berwick Street, is the old **Empire Office Building |9|**, now transformed into a dynamic centre for Queensland's more experimental multi-arts organisations. The interior of the building has recently been gutted and completely rebuilt and, as well as shops, cafés and offices, contains a multi-function purpose built performance space that is used by all the building's tenants. Expressions Dance Company, Kooemba Jdarra Theatre Company (a Murri organisation), Rock'n'Roll Circus and the Elision Contemporary Music Ensemble are some of the companies occupying the building. This people-friendly venue is an important part of the emerging cultural precinct in both Fortitude Valley and New Farm, and takes its place proudly alongside the Brisbane City Council's Powerhouse development down on the river at New Farm (See Walk 11).

A row of funky shops selling retro clothing and alternative books occupies the block between McLachlan Street and Ann Street, and some of the cafés here are very tempting. Otherwise continue along Brunswick Street to Ann Street, where the **Empire Hotel |10|** (see Walk No. 5) offers everything from loud music to the bizarre elegance of the Press Club Bar. A short left-hand detour into Ann Street will take you to the **Institute of Modern Art |11|**.

Opening Times

Most shops open Mon–Fri 9am–5pm, and Sat 9am–4pm. Galleries are usually closed on Sunday and Monday.
Fusions Gallery: corner Brunswick and Malt streets (3358 5122)
Philip Bacon Gallery:
2 Arthur Street (3358 3555)
Gallery 482:
482 Brunswick Street (3254 0933)
Fox Galleries:
482 Brunswick Street (3254 3155)
Jan Murphy Gallery:
486 Brunswick Street (3254 1855)
Institute of Modern Art:
608 Ann Street (3252 5750)
Fire-Works Gallery:
678 Ann Street (3216 1250)
Celestial Glass Studio and Gallery:
corner Ann and Brookes streets
(3852 2385)
Bellas Gallery: corner James and Robertson streets (3252 1608)
Doggett Street Studio:
85 Doggett Street (3252 9292)

Refreshments

There is a wide choice of cafés, pubs and restaurants. Most are open 7 days a week until late.

Walk back down Ann Street, against the flow of the traffic and away from the city, resisting the temptations of the Brunswick Street Mall, which are included in Walk No. 5. Continue to No. 678 Ann Street, where **Fire-Works Gallery |12|** specialises in indigenous art, artefacts and clothing of high quality. The works of the world-renowned northern Australian Murri painter Emily Kame Kngwarreye are exhibited here, as well as screen-printed fabrics and clothing from Jimmy Pike. And for some nostalgic shopping, there's nothing more retro than the Lifeline and Brisbane City Mission shops next door.

Coffee breaks

For more art galleries, continue down Ann Street to the corner of Brookes Street, where it's not uncommon to see artists at work in the **Celestial Glass Studio |13|**. Retrace your steps and proceed down James Street on the left where **Merlo's coffee factory |14|** on the corner of McLachlan Street roasts beans daily between 8.30am and 12.30pm. You can purchase an extensive selection of beans here, or sit at a huge wooden table in the converted warehouse and drink the freshest coffee you're likely to have all day.

Thus fortified, you'll be ready to face another gallery, the **Bellas |15|**, two blocks along on the corner of Robertson Street. Then continue along James Street and turn left into Arthur Street. If you have had your fill of art galleries by this time repair to the **Queen's Arms Hotel |16|** on the corner.

Wynberg, residence of the Roman Catholic Archbishop

Dating from 1883, it is possibly the oldest pub in this district. As the pub's T-shirt used to say, 'Prince Charles had his first drink in the Queen's Arms'.

Otherwise, keep going along Arthur Street, where old Queensland houses mingle more or less happily with modern town houses. Some of the best are Nos. 201 and 199 on the right side, at the corner of Chester Street, and No. 217 which has been prettified in shades of lavender. On the left side, notice Nos. 222 and 224, both recently renovated, and further along, high above a cutting on the rock face on the right, is **one of the earliest houses in the district |17|**.

When you reach Commercial Road, turn left. Here is a fine example of the way old warehouses are being tuned into apartment buildings – the Primary Producers' Co-operative has taken on a new lease of life as Teneriffe Apartments.

Gentrification has brought a new emphasis to this once-derelict part of Brisbane, and antique shops and cafés are changing the character of the area. As you turn into Commercial Road, notice Far Pavilions, with unusual imported furniture. But it's time for another art gallery, so turn right into Doggett Street and continue to the end to find the **Doggett Street Studio |18|** at No. 85. This is the last gallery on the Fortitude Valley Art Circuit, so turn left into Longland Street, from where it is only three blocks to Ann Street. From here you can catch a bus back into the city.

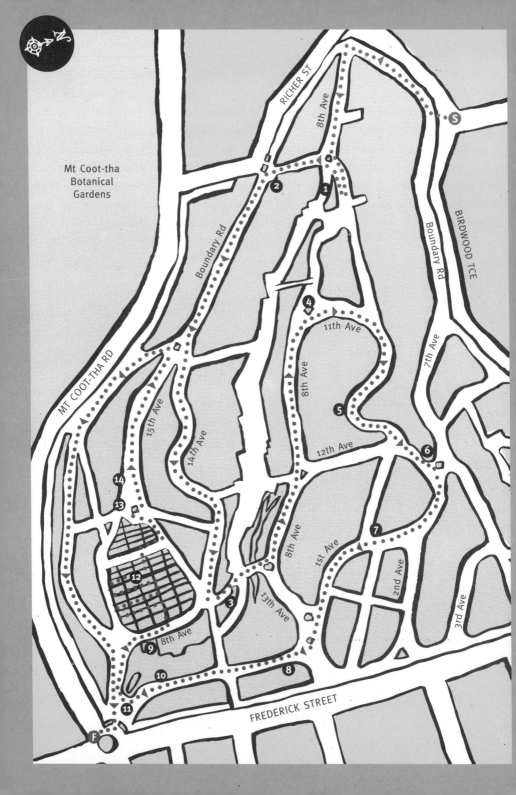

Toowong Cemetery
The peaceful dead

Start

City Bus 410 from the corner of Adelaide and Albert Streets, to stop 30 on the top boundary of the cemetery in Birdwood Terrace. Note that this is not the main entrance.

Finish

Main cemetery gate. Any bus back into the city from stop 14 in Milton Road.

Length/Time

4.5 km/2 hours

Tips & access

There are many hills and valleys, and the walking can at times be strenuous. Sturdy shoes are essential, as well as a water bottle and a hat. Many of the older trees have roots that have spread out over the paths, so be careful not to stumble. The areas around the main entrance gate are the most accessible for wheelchairs and bicycles.

Cemeteries are not just for the morbid. An old burial ground can be a mine of historical information, a haven of tranquillity in the midst of a busy city or, as the poet Philip Larkin said, 'a place to grow more wise in, if only that so many dead lie round'. Toowong Cemetery is one of the oldest in Brisbane, a 57 hectare site with over 115,000 graves dating back to 1871. This walk concentrates on the Victorian monuments and the graves with heritage value, but also takes in the more modern and colourful areas of Russian and Greek Orthodox graves, and the Jewish section.

Walk key

1. Small Chinese section | 2. Miniature Greek village church | 3. Military graves | 4. Shelter shed, and public toilets | 5. Roman Catholic gravestones | 6. Celtic graves | 7. Memorial to tiny infants and still-born babies | 8. Jewish section | 9. Sexton's Office Museum | 10. Soldiers' Memorial | 11. Temple of Peace | 12. Heritage graves | 13. Samuel Wensley Blackall | 14. Sir Samuel Walker Griffith

From bus stop 30, walk back a few metres where you will find a short track through the bush perimeter strip to Boundary Road, which runs along the top of the cemetery. From here there is a sweeping view of the city and suburbs.

Chinese and Greek graves

Turn right, go down the hill a little way, and take 8th Avenue on the left. This leads down a short avenue of eucalypts to a massive spreading fig tree. Beyond this is the **small Chinese section** |1| of the cemetery on the right, a favourite place for the local Chinese community to do their Tai Chi exercises early in the morning. The Chinese graves are distinctive because the headstones all face west.

After exploring this section, return to the fig tree and turn left into 9th Avenue, going up the hill and turning left again into Boundary Road, which runs along the top of a low ridge.

This road is flanked by Greek and Russian Orthodox graves, their double and triple crosses often inset with portraits of the deceased. The most imposing memorial here, on the left as you begin the walk along 9th Avenue, takes the form of a **miniature Greek village church** |2|.

At the end of this path there is a shelter for which by now you will probably be grateful. Veer left into 14th Avenue and follow its curves as far as the T-junction, then turn again left onto a road leading to a creek crossing. There are a number of **military graves** |3| on the right.

A hundred metres along is another T-junction. Take the left fork, following the road which then continues as 8th Avenue. At the junction of this road with 11th Avenue there is another shelter shed, and some **public toilets** |4|.

Turn into 11th Avenue, which winds up the hill to a line of pines on the right; just past these trees are some very ornate **Roman Catholic gravestones** |5| and further up, on the left, past the junction with 12th Avenue, is an interesting group of **Celtic graves** |6|.

Continue to the top of the rise as far as the shelter shed, and turn right into 2nd Avenue. Soon after this, take the right fork into 1st Avenue which goes down the hill. Here, a little way down on the right, is a moving **memorial to tiny infants and stillborn babies** |7|.

The cemetery museum and the Temple of Peace

At the foot of the hill turn right past the small shelter shed into Boundary Road, which leads past the **Jewish section** |8| on the left, near the perimeter fence. Next is the **Sexton's Office Museum** |9| (see Opening Times), where you can pick up the Brisbane City Council's Heritage Trail booklet, which gives full details of the historical graves you will pass during the rest of the walk. The Sexton's Office also contains some old historic photographs and you may be able to get a copy of a booklet interpreting the symbolism of the Victorian monumental masonry.

From the Sexton's Office, walk towards the main entrance gate past the **Soldiers' Memorial** |10|, unveiled on Anzac Day 1924, where there is a Cross of Sacrifice and a 10-tonne block of Helidon sandstone forming the Stone of Remembrance.

But the most bizarre and one of the most moving monuments in the cemetery is the **Temple of Peace** |11|, on the left as you face the main gate. Built by Richard Ramo, it is dedicated to world peace, and commemorates his three sons who were killed in the First World War, as well as his adopted son Fred who, as the memorial says, died of a misplaced love. There is some mystery about the circumstances of Fred's death in 1923 – the official verdict said was that it was an accidental shooting, but one old lady who knew the family well has her doubts. Ramo became bitter to the point of paranoia, and included in the memorial a plaque to his dog, which he states was 'maliciously poisoned'. The Temple of Peace, with its elaborate symbolism and intricate coloured lead-lighted glass, draws tourists, members of the Industrial Workers of the World and many pacifists. It has been given heritage status by the National Trust of Queensland.

Just behind the Temple of Peace are two war memorial graves, and near the roadside opposite the Soldiers' Memorial you will find the grave of Edward McGregor (1862–1939), whose marble representation sits on top of his monument clasping a laurel wreath. No other inmate of the cemetery is commemorated in a statue.

Opening Times

The main gates and the Birdwood Terrace entry are never closed.
The Sexton's Office Museum: Mon–Fri, 7am–4pm, except Wed, 9am–3.30pm.

Refreshments

Water taps only.

Route Notes

The Brisbane City Council Heritage Trail booklet No. 5, Toowong Cemetery, gives more detailed descriptions of many of the graves. It is available free of charge from Brisbane City Council Customer Service Centres.

There are public toilets near the office at the main gates, and at the shed at the junction of 8th and 11th Avenues.

Heritage graves

Go back towards the Soldiers' Memorial and cross 8th Avenue, keeping to the left of the toilet block, to find the **Heritage graves** |12| (From here the walk roughly follows the route of the City Council Heritage booklet.) In a prominent position, as befits the family that designed and made about 70 per cent of the earliest headstones and monuments in the cemetery, are the graves of the pioneering Petrie family, descendants of Andrew Petrie (not buried here), the first free settler in the district and founder of Brisbane's oldest firm of monumental masons, whose stonemason's business operated across the road from the main gate until 1981. His oldest son John was Brisbane's first mayor, and his grandson Andrew a member of the Legislative Assembly for 33 years.

Toowong Cemetery

The late 19th century was a time of high infant mortality in Brisbane, for sanitation was poor and there were many accidental deaths. Two plots along from the Petrie graves, on the left, lie the four young children of the Horsfall family, as well as a mysterious child labelled simply 'Little Jack'.

Take the path to the left between two pine trees. Just past the grave of Annie McCreedy turn left again and follow the path to the graves of three pioneer children, one of whom was the son of the settlement's first schoolteacher, Esther Roberts. Turn right here and climb up the hill, noticing the elaborate headstones in this section of the cemetery. Depending on time and your own interests, you can continue straight up the hill, or wander off through the paths on the right, to see some of the other graves described in the City Council booklet.

A pioneer medical family, the Bancrofts, are buried on the right halfway up the hill, and four paths further along on the right is the elaborate monument to Robert Russell Smellie, who established an engineering business in Brisbane in the 1860s.

At the corner of the fourth path on the right after R. R. Smellie's monument are the draped mourning urns of the Raff family, early politicians and pastoralists.

Two rows further along, past the pine tree, turn right at the grave of Kenneth Hutchinson, and look on the right for the graves of Thomas Finney and James Isles, who were founders of one of Brisbane's oldest drapery businesses, together in death as they were in life.

There are many elaborate monuments along this path including, on the left-hand side, that of soldier Sir Maurice O'Connell, who was the grandson of William Bligh and a founding member of the Queensland Legislative Council.

Senior citizens

At the end of this path turn left at the grave of Dorothy Hawthorn, and follow the path up the hill as it winds to the left, to the dominant grave of the cemetery, that of **Samuel Wensley Blackall |13|**, second governor of Queensland. He chose his own site in the cemetery, and was the first person to be buried here.

Anticlockwise from Blackall's monument is the modest grave of the great Queenslander **Sir Samuel Walker Griffith |14|**, not just a local politician but one of the founding fathers of Australian Federation and the Constitution. His gravestone may well be modest in appearance, but the list of his achievements is impressive.

Spend a few minutes on Blackall's Hill, for it offers a fine view of Brisbane and is an ideal place for quiet reflection. Then take the path behind the Blackall memorial, following 15th Avenue along the crest of the ridge. This is a pleasantly wooded part of the cemetery, and the path wanders through a variety of interesting graves which date from the early part of this century. There are also excellent views of Stuartholme Convent School.

When you come to Boundary Road, turn left and follow it down the hill to the cemetery gates. From here, turn left and cross Frederick Street into Milton Road, walk past the car sales yard and the service station on the left, and catch any bus back into the city from stop 14.

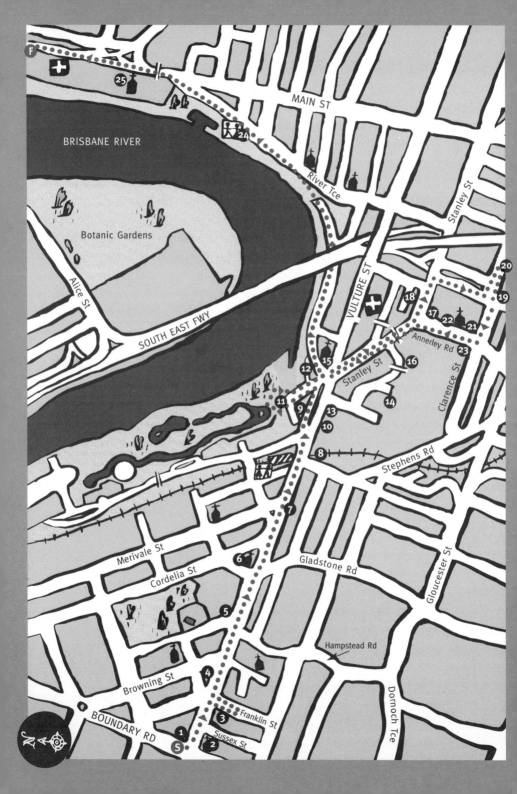

South Brisbane

Brisbane's stately rival

Start

Corner of Boundary and
Vulture Streets, West End.
City Bus 190 Adelaide and
George Streets, to stop 7.

Finish

St Mary's Anglican Church,
Main Street Kangaroo Point, City
Bus 475, 476. For a longer walk
cross the Story Bridge to the CBD

Length/Time

5.5 km/1.5 hours
8 km/2.5–3 hours

Access

Quite flat, except for a hilly
stretch in Merton Road.

Like many parts of Brisbane,
South Brisbane grew into a prosperous
borough during the boom of the 1880s,
its only rival being the City of Brisbane
across the river. A centre for transport
and industry, South Brisbane was
also home to some of the wealthier
merchant families, and this walk
gives an indication of the way the
area developed until it was raised
to the status of a City in 1903.
In 1925, however, it lost its separate
status when it amalgamated with
its rival across the river to form
Greater Brisbane.

Walk key

1. Boundary Street/Vulture Street intersection | 2. Uniting Church | 3. Three similar early houses |
4. An elaborate old house | 5. Brisbane State High School | 6. St Andrew's Anglican Church |
7. Serbian Orthodox Church | 8. Somerville House | 9. South Brisbane Memorial Park |
10. Cumbooquepa | 11. The Ship Inn | 12. Queensland Maritime Museum | 13. South Brisbane
Town Hall | 14. St Laurence's College | 15. South Brisbane Library | 16. Mater Hospital |
17. Clarence Corner Hotel | 18. Nos. 609–617 Stanley Street | 19. Holy Trinity Anglican Church |
20. Russian Orthodox Church of St Seraphim | 21. Bethany Gospel Hall | 22. Princess Theatre |
23. Mater Private Hospital | 24. lookout | 25. St Mary's Anglican Church

The walk begins at the busy **Boundary Street/Vulture Street intersection |1|** at West End, a suburb of great charm and ethnic diversity.

Get off the bus in Boundary Street, turn left into Vulture Street and walk east along the left side of the road. Opposite is the ornate cream and red brick **Uniting Church |2|**, and ahead on the corner with Besant Street, a rare old shop with wide awnings wrapping around the corner.

Cross Vulture Street now, to go up Franklin Street to see, on the right side, **three similar early houses |3|** that have been stunningly restored. The attractive timber fretwork under the gables and iron lace verandahs are wonderful examples of the decorative architecture of bygone days.

Away from Vulture Street

At the corner of Browning Street, notice **an elaborate old house |4|**, now restored and partly modified as professional offices. Past here look left and uphill across a bare allotment to a grand old mansion, with a rectangular ridge cap made of iron lace.

Next on the left and taking up the whole block is **Brisbane State High School |5|**, Queensland's most highly regarded state school, and across Ernest Street is the solid mellow stone edifice of **St Andrew's Anglican Church |6|**.

Pause under the shady mango tree ahead to look across at the quaint **Serbian Orthodox Church |7|**, its two cupolas giving it an exotic eastern appearance.

Parks and mansions

Further along at Stephens Road are the red brick buildings of the old part of **Somerville House |8|**, a prestigious private school for girls, which takes up the next block. At this point Vulture Street crosses the railway line, and the second set of steps leads down to the drinking fountain and toilets on the railway platform.

A little way ahead is the delightfully cool and shaded **South Brisbane Memorial Park |9|**. Take the curved path that follows the direction of Vulture Street. On the left is a memorial with a First World War anti-aircraft gun and, at the foot of the stairs, a very early drinking fountain with drinking bowls for dogs at the base.

Look across Vulture Street to **Cumbooquepa |10|** (from the local Murri word for a group of waterholes), built in 1890 by Thomas Blacket Stephens. Cumbooquepa now forms the core of Somerville House which took over the property in 1919.

Take the path leading sharp left at the big fig tree and follow the top outer boundary of the park. This leads to a flight of stone steps, marked by a decorative sign over pillars made of green and pink porphyry, a local stone also known as Brisbane tuff. At the bottom of these steps is the **Ship Inn |11|** (1870) in its pretty modern precinct, where you may be tempted to stop and rest. This part of the river once boasted a thriving port, and the hotel was a Mecca for thirsty sailors. Opposite the hotel is the **Queensland Maritime Museum |12|** (see Opening Times).

It's worth spending five or ten minutes wandering around the Ship Inn precinct before you walk back along the lower wall of the park, past the First World War memorial to Vulture Street.

From the retaining wall of the park you can see across the road, next to Somerville House, the brick and sandstone tower of the old **South Brisbane Town Hall |13|**. Built in 1892 in the Italianate Classical Revival style, like so many buildings of this period, financial difficulties delayed its completion until 1904, when the clock was finally installed.

Up on the hill behind the Town Hall is a large red and white building, part of the Christian Brothers' school known as **St Laurence's College |14|**.

On the left, on the corner of Dock Street, is the old **South Brisbane Library |15|**, built in three stages. The left part of the building, the old South Brisbane Post and Telegraph Office, was erected some time before 1882. A new wing with the square turreted tower was added when it was taken over by the South Brisbane Mechanics Institute in 1894 for use as a School of Arts.

Stanley Street

Cross Dock Street, then Vulture Street, to Stanley Street on the right. The building on the corner is the old Bank of New South Wales, built in the early 1920s, when this street was an important centre of commerce. The building is now used as private offices.

Stanley Street is now dominated by the **Mater Hospital |16|** on the right, and the

Opening Times

Maritime Museum: Mon–Sun 9.30am–5pm

Refreshments

Cafés are plentiful in West End at the start of the walk. There is a drinking fountain at the Vulture Street Railway Station, and the Ship Inn at South Bank is open all day, as is the Clarence Corner Hotel in Stanley Street.

Route Notes

The end of this walk joins up with the Kangaroo Point cliff-top walk, No.16. Together they make a half-day expedition. There are drinking fountains and toilets at Vulture Street Railway Station.

Mater Medical Centre on the left. Past Water Street on the left, at the corner of Annerley Road, Nos. 596–614 Stanley Street date from the widening of Stanley Street in 1927. The buildings here are remarkable for the verandahs extending out over the street.

Continue along Stanley Street, noticing as you go the **Clarence Corner Hotel |17|** across the road. In February 1865, the *Brisbane Courier* (then priced fourpence)

advertised for private sale 'That First-class HOTEL known as the CLARENCE HOTEL, Stanley-street, South Brisbane, at the junction of the Old and New Ipswich Roads, and doing a splendid business. At present let for 6 pounds per week, for two years.'

The hotel has been known variously as The Clarence (1864), The Newtown (1929), The Clarence Corner (1965) and The Colonial Inn Hotel (1988). Rugby Union fans who now claim it for their own call it The Clarence Corner. League fans are not welcome – the famous Bill McLean, who used to own the pub, once got into a punch-up with some league supporters. The night his son and nephew were named as members of the Wallaby team, they made improper suggestions about gentlemen's football. Blood was spilled, they say.

Continuing along Stanley Street, notice the row of shops from **Nos. 609–617 |18|** with their flamboyant central pediments, and the residential flats above them. The next two shops date back to the 1860s, and the Phoenix Buildings, six two-storey rendered masonry shops on the corner of Merton Road, were designed by an illustrious local architect in 1889. While looking at the buildings across the road, don't miss the decorative details of the shop you are walking past – the entrances lined with marble and tile, leadlight panels above the doors, and especially the pressed metal ceiling of No. 610.

Cross Stanley Street at the Hotel Morrison and walk up Merton Road, a residential street which gives a clear indication of how

Russian Orthodox Church

the working class lived in the early 19th century. The cottage at No. 45 is remarkable, with its gable roof and lattice work.

Religion and theatre

Turn left into Hawthorne Street and go steeply uphill to the Spanish Mission style church on the right. **Holy Trinity Anglican Church |19|** was built in 1930 at the beginning of the Depression. It is said that the site was used for religious ceremonies long before white settlement, as a Murri bora ring. A little further along Hawthorne Street is the **Russian Orthodox Church of St Seraphim |20|**.

Retrace your steps along Hawthorne Street and turn left into Merton Road again. Almost immediately opposite is

Catherine Street, which has a number of old workers' cottages and leads through to Annerley Road.

Turn right into Annerley Road and walk along past the **Bethany Gospel Hall |21|**. Beyond a small shopping complex is the exquisite **Princess Theatre |22|**, the oldest surviving theatre building in Brisbane. This ornate Italianate building constructed as a theatre in 1888 has a chequered past. Only a few productions were staged in the 1890s, and they had to compete with a clothing business in the dress circle. It has been used as a cinema showing silent films and as a stove factory and, when the Yankees arrived during the Second World War, the Princess became the administrative and rehearsal centre for their entertainment unit.

Films continued to be shown there until 1948, and Murri elder Lorna Bligh, who lived on Annerley Road in the postwar period, has vivid memories of going to the pictures there in a big gang every Friday and Saturday night. The future of the building is again in doubt but it is listed on the State Heritage Register and cannot be demolished.

Across the road from the Princess Theatre is the Mater Hill hospital precinct, the original hospital built for the Sisters of Mercy by prominent architect Robin Dods. In 1893 the sisters purchased the five acres of land for seven thousand pounds, and in 1910 the private hospital was opened and blessed, followed a year later by the public part of the hospital. The old **Mater Private |23|** is no longer used by patients, but a walk through the grounds gives a good view of its highly ornamented construction.

The river connection

Turn left into Stanley Street, and walk back on the left side of the road until you come to the Vulture Street intersection. Cross the road here and walk down Dock Street to the river where the old dry dock (more properly known as a graving dock) forms part of the Queensland Maritime Museum (also included in Walk No.4).

Just past the graving dock, Dock Street becomes Lower River Terrace, which follows the river bank under the freeway. To reach the top of Kangaroo Point cliffs, take the left fork of Ellis Street. Some little way up is a walking path to a **lookout |24|**, with fine views across the river to the City Botanic Gardens and the CBD.

Continue along the top of the cliffs on River Terrace until it joins Main Street at the South Bank TAFE College. Under the footbridge on the left, a steep drive goes up to **St Mary's Anglican Church |25|**, where the first governors of the colony used to worship. There is also a very fine rectory and, from the church grounds, another commanding view of the Botanical Gardens and the financial sector of the city.

There is a bus stop for the city outside Mt Olivet Hospice, next to the church. Or walk another 2.5 kilometres across the Story Bridge, always worth doing for the exciting views, into the city, turning left past All Hallows Convent and walking down Ann Street.

Walk key

1. 249 Lutwyche Road |
2. War Memorial |
3. Windsor Council Chambers | 4. Windsor Substation | 5. Porphyry quarry | 6. Flower Street | 7. Kirkston | 8. Brick gate posts | 9. No. 38 Palmer Street | 10. Windsor Primary School | 11. No. 86 Constitution Road | 12. No. 66 Constitution Road | 13. No. 30 Constitution Road | 14. Windsor Railway Station | 15. Downey Park | 16. Little bridge over Enoggera Creek

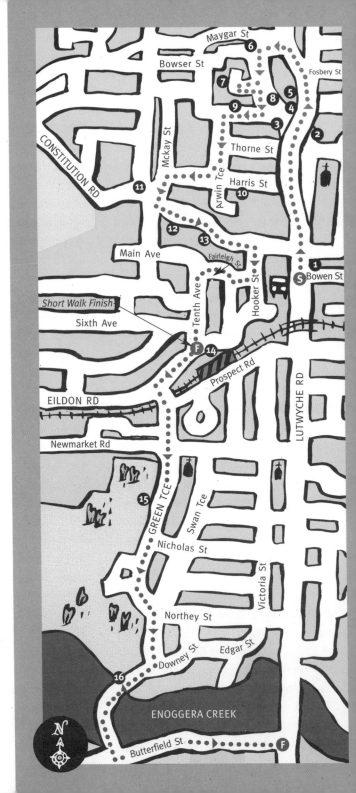

Windsor

Porphyry and tuff

Start

Lutwyche Road, on the corner of Bowen Street. City Bus 321 from Edward Street in the city, 379 from Adelaide Street, or 334 from Elizabeth Street, to stop 14.

Finish

Windsor Railway Station in Eildon Road (short walk), or Bowen Bridge Road (longer walk).

Length/Time

2.5–3 km/1 hour
4.5 km/1.5 hours

Access & Tips

This is a hilly part of Brisbane, so stout walking shoes are essential. Take a bottle of water as there are few refreshment stops. The very steep hills make it difficult, but not impossible for wheelchair users.

Almost every Australian city has a suburb called Windsor, and the Brisbane version probably got its name because the hilly landscape reminded homesick settlers of the land around Windsor Castle. This may also be the reason why the first white settlers called the Murri inhabitants the Duke of York's clan. Although Windsor is less than 5 kilometres from the CBD, Breakfast Creek and the dense bushland made a formidable barrier in the early days of settlement, and so the first white settlers were tradesmen lured by the rich clay soil, rather than people seeking to create a desirable residential area. Brickyards, tanneries and quarries were the first industries in the 1850s, and once Bowen Bridge was constructed in 1862 development went ahead very quickly. Today the suburb is a comprehensive mix of historical beauty and faded glamour, and this walk gives a good overview of its many charms.

Take the bus to Lutwyche Road, stop 14, and cross to the corner of Bowen Street. The first building of historical interest is at **249 Lutwyche Road** |1|, now just a sad shadow (or perhaps a gaudy reminder) of its former self. Once called the Tapestry Cottage, it was originally built as a hotel, but was never granted a licence. It has had many incarnations during its lifetime, including one as a butcher's shop with slaughter yards at the back. It is now a home entertainment store painted in garish colours, which may have frightened away the two friendly ghosts reported to have lived there.

Walk along Lutwyche Road past Roblane Street, where a tiny park marks the site of the old Bowen Bridge Road State School, opened in 1865. The number of students soon outgrew the little building and moved across the road to the Windsor State School, but the park remains as a **War Memorial** |2|, with a particularly impressive monument of Helidon sandstone.

The monument recalls the 125 soldiers from Windsor who died in this war, more than ten per cent of the total contingent, and so proud were the citizens of their fallen husbands and sons that the Windsor Town Council, as it was then, willingly gave £1,300 to erect this memorial.

Pink porphyry

Re-cross Lutwyche Road here, and just opposite and below the Albion Road turnoff you will see the old **Windsor Council Chambers** |3|, built in 1897 of local pink porphyry stone dressed with sandstone. When the shire became a town in 1904, the workmen seem to have had neither the time nor the inclination to carve a new stone, so they filled in the word 'Shire' with cement and carved 'Town' across the top. Unfortunately the filling didn't stay put, and soon the word 'Shire' was on full display again, creating confusion for people insistent on historical accuracy, but adding considerably to the building's charm. The garden is particularly attractive and contains weeping figs and palms as well as colourful flower beds.

The **Windsor Substation** |4| comes next. It was built in 1948 to provide extra electrical power to the trams which used this road until the system was dismantled in the 1960s. Brisbane residents have never forgotten their trams and there are moves afoot to restore a service linking some parts of the city and suburbs, although the Windsor Substation will probably never regain its original function.

Just behind the Substation, on the corner of Rupert Street, are the remains of the old **porphyry quarry** |5| which supplied most of the stone for the buildings in this area. The hill from which this quarry was cut used to slope right down to Albion Road.

Go to the lights at the corner of Maygar Street and turn left. Walk up the steep incline of **Flower Street** |6| (first on the left), where some houses of a later period, the 1920s and 1930s, are evidence that Windsor remained a prime residential area for many years, largely because of the ready availability of stone and brick, and the elevated building sites which caught every breath of wind on still summer days.

Top of the town

No. 21 Flower Street is a good example of this period, as is No. 27, with its fine tall Alexander palms and its pleasant outlook over the quarry. Halfway along Flower Street on the right is the cul-de-sac of Rupert Street, where at No. 23 stands one of the finest houses in the district, the two-storey brick and timber **Kirkston** |7|.

Built in 1889, it commands superb views from its protruding upper balconies, and has recently been restored to its original magnificence, although some people may find the modern lead lighting disturbingly out of period. Among the fine details are mellow brickwork, timber pillars topped by carved brackets, iron lace, and a rare slate roof with double chimneys and terracotta chimneypots – nights can get nippy in July, even in Brisbane.

Return to Flower Street, turn right and walk down to the two **brick gate posts** |8| which were once the entrance to Kirkston. The City Council Heritage Trail booklet tells the well-known story of John Flower, the solicitor who built Kirkston and after whom the street is named. His habit was to reward the first child to reach the gates and open them, by tossing a penny into the eager crowd as gaily as any French aristocrat. From here there is also a different view of the pretty pink porphyry Council Chambers. Turn right into Palmer Street (named after

Refreshments

No cafés or hotels.

Route Notes

The area is very hilly. Be sure to take a water bottle, as no drinks are available along the way.

Sir Arthur Palmer, Premier of Queensland from 1870–74) and walk uphill, noting especially the galvanised iron roof, ridge cap and finials of **No. 38 |9|**, and some lovely houses from the 1920s on both sides of the street.

Turn left into Arwin Terrace, and note the two interesting houses on the right just before you turn right into Harris Street. Take a left turn into Mackay Street and, towards the top of the hill, look left for a view of the red brick **Windsor Primary School |10|** , which was built in 1916 by a former pupil, M.R.Hornibrook, who was also responsible for the Hornibrook Highway to the Redcliffe Peninsula. Even in 1919 it had a massive enrolment of over a thousand pupils.

At Constitution Road turn left, where old and new buildings sit together in reasonable harmony. The mustard-coloured townhouse on the right at **No. 86 |11|** is particularly striking.

Houses of the 1880s

There are some splendid old houses in this street: **No. 66 |12|**, once called Kensington and built in 1889 of brick and timber, is not easy to see behind its white picket fence, but it has an unusual second storey at the back, cut into the hill. Like many grand old houses it declined in status, falling victim to the dreadful 1950s custom of enclosing verandahs and dividing the living areas into cheap flats, but it was lovingly restored in the 1980s, as Brisbane began to take pride in its historic buildings

Windsor Council Chambers

once again. During its most dilapidated period it took on a new role as the local haunted house, although there is no evidence to support these claims.

Keep going down Constitution Road, keeping an eye out for Nos. 61 and 57 on the left, just below Kensington, both carefully restored and with views of the city. This is a particularly fine area, with most of the houses probably looking better now than when they were built. It is one of the most desirable streets in Windsor.

At **No. 30 Constitution Road |13|** is Fairleigh, almost a decade older than Kensington. It used to be twice its present size, but during the First World War it was divided into two separate buildings, one of which was moved onto the old croquet lawn facing Fairleigh Street in the next block.

This second house unfortunately burned down in the 1950s.

Keep going to Hooker Street, opposite the Windsor Primary School, turn right and then almost immediately right again into Fairleigh Street, which once marked the border of the Fairleigh estate. A short way along, on a bend, is a pretty little house which used to be the kitchen section of the original Fairleigh. The old greenhouse, which has also been converted into a separate house, stands behind Fairleigh but is not easily seen from the road.

Turn left down Tenth Avenue, and left again into Eildon Road. A short way along is the **Windsor Railway Station |14|** for the trip back to the CBD.

Through the park

For a longer walk through parklands, turn right into Eildon Road from Tenth Avenue, then take the first left into Cox Road across the railway line. When you cross Newmarket Road at the lights, Cox Road becomes Green Terrace, which eventually swings in a curve beside **Downey Park |15|**. Keep following Green Terrace, turn right into Downey Street at the T-junction, cross the little bridge over **Enoggera Creek |16|**, and follow the cycle path to Butterfield Street. Turn left and walk down to the big intersection with Bowen Bridge Road, with a service station on the left and the Royal Brisbane Hospital on the right. Cross the road to catch a bus back into the city.

Walk key

1. Hamilton reach of the Brisbane River |
2. Cremorne |
3. No. 39 Eldernell Terrace, Bishopsbourne |
4. No. 48 Eldernell Terrace |
5. No. 66 Markwell Street, Berrimilla | 6. Woollahra |
7. Hamilton Town Hall |
8. St Augustine's Anglican Church | 9. Nos. 9 and 10 Charlton Street | 10. Nos. 31 and 23 Killara Avenue |
11. Bayuda | 12. Killara |
13. No. 100 Crescent Road, Myrtleville | 14. Cooksley's house | 15. Palma Rosa |
16. Toorak | 17. No. 16 Toorak Road, Briamon |
18. Cameron's Rocks |
19. Newstead House |
20. Breakfast Creek Hotel

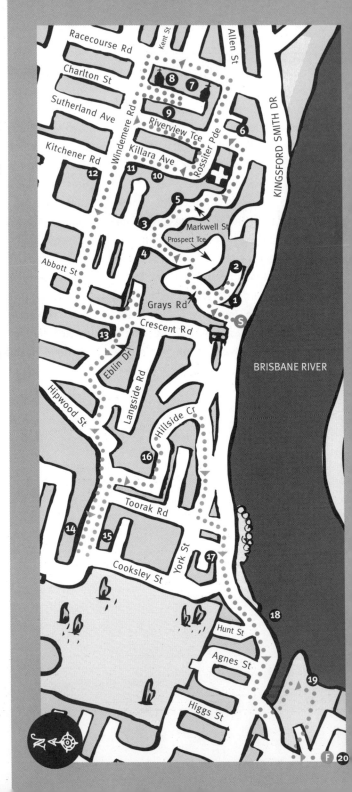

BRISBANE RIVER

Hamilton

High life on the hill

Start

Corner of Kingsford Smith Drive
and Grays Road. City Bus 300,
301 from corner of Adelaide
and Edward Streets, or 302
from Elizabeth Street.
CityCat to Hamilton Wharf.

Finish

Shorter walk – Kingsford Smith
Drive and Toorak Road.
Longer walk – Newstead House
at Breakfast Creek.

Length/Time

6.5 km/2.25 hours
7.5 km/2.5 hours

Access

The initial part of this
walk involves a very steep
climb up to Hamilton Heights,
and another steep descent
down Toorak Road. The steep
hills make it difficult, but
not impossible for
wheelchair users.

These days it is home to the rich and powerful, but the suburb of Hamilton sits firmly on convict foundations. Kingsford Smith Drive, the main road which links the city and the airport, was hewn out of the rocky cliffs along the side of the river by felons, who also cleared most of the land for housing. Now the inhabitants of the grand mansions enjoy cool breezes, wonderful views, and the satisfaction of knowing they live in the most elite suburb in Brisbane. This walk includes the major public buildings of the district and some of the most important domestic dwellings, which cover a range of architectural styles including Tudor and Gothic revival, Federation, Queensland vernacular, and Spanish Mission.

Take the bus to stop 17 and enjoy a view of the **Hamilton reach of the Brisbane River |1|** before turning left into Grays Road. If coming by CityCat, turn left and walk back towards the city, taking the second turn on the right into Grays Road.

From Grays Road, take the first turning on the right into Mullens Street, and walk to No. 34 at the end, a magnificent old house called **Cremorne |2|**, built in 1905 and occupied by the same family ever since. It is remarkable not just for its position, which gives it uninterrupted views of the river, but for its wide verandahs with octagonal rotundas at each end graced with dome-shaped roofs.

Of bishops and builders

Return down Mullens Street, turn right back into Grays Road, right into Prospect Terrace at the top, then left into Eldernell Terrace, lined with magnificent old trees. Veer right until you come to the entrance of **No. 39, Bishopsbourne |3|**, the residence of the Anglican archbishop of Brisbane.

The house was originally called Eldernell, a name with a more prosaic provenance than one might suspect. The first owner wanted to call it after his wife Nell, but as their daughter bore the same name, he had to differentiate between them. The house dates from 1869, although the private chapel just inside the gates is modern.

Across the road and just along on the left at **No. 48 |4|** is the house designed for himself in 1923 by Brisbane architect Lange Powell. He was also responsible for the

Masonic Temple and St Martin's House in Ann Street (see Walk No. 3, Wickham Terrace and City Churches). The fanlight over the door is typical of the Georgian revival style, and the shuttered sash windows are particularly fine. It is said that Powell designed the whole house around the bronze door knocker which he brought back from the Deep South of America.

Turn right now into Markwell Street, which winds down the hill past many remarkable houses, the most interesting being a timber house called **Berrimilla** at **No. 66 |5|**, one of the earliest Federation style houses in the area, with its ornamental brackets, wide verandahs and iron lace balustrades. Markwell Street ends at Wyenbah Terrace, which offers excellent views of the Gateway Bridge.

At the end of Wyenbah Street turn left into the appropriately named Riverview Terrace, and follow it up to Rossiter Parade where you turn right.

A little way along, on the right again, is Lexington Terrace, and on the corner at No. 1 is **Woollahra |6|** (1888), a very pretty two-storey house with cast-iron roof finials, ridge cap and column brackets. This is a good example of English architecture modified to suit the Queensland climate; in a period when no distinctive local style had yet developed, verandahs to catch the breeze were being added to English designs.

Racecourse Road

Go back into Rossiter Parade, continue in the same direction and turn left into Racecourse Road. There are plenty of coffee shops here, most of which have toilets attached. Walk along Racecourse Road away from the river and pass the **Hamilton Town Hall** |7| (1920s), a red brick building roofed with locally manufactured glazed tiles. It is now used as a Public Library.

Roughly opposite Balowrie Street, on the left side of the road, are the park-like grounds of **St Augustine's Anglican Church** |8|, a brick building erected in thanksgiving for the Empire's victory in the First World War. The tower commemorates the people who served in the Second World War, although it was not erected until 1961. The church contains some of artist William Bustard's most beautiful stained glass windows, and the bell in the grounds is believed to date back to the year 320 AD, when the emperor Constantine hung it in a Romanian church. It's a good story!

Continue along Racecourse Road to the junction with Windemere Road, turn left, and then left again into Charlton Street. Almost every house in this area is worth a glance, but **Nos. 9 and 10 Charlton Street** |9| probably have the greatest heritage interest – No. 9 was originally the rectory for St Augustine's church, and No. 10, built in 1904 and originally called Wiembilla, is a typical example of the Federation style which was common to this period of history.

Charlton Street is a dead-end, so retrace your steps and turn left into Windemere Road. No. 132 was built in 1928, an example of the Tudor revival style now very much out of fashion, as Queenslanders

Opening Times

Newstead House: Mon–Fri 10am–4pm, Sun 2pm–5pm.

Refreshments

Brett's Wharf, just past the CityCat terminal, is good for elegant food with a view of the river. Less expensive food can be bought at the cafés in Racecourse Road, or at the **Breakfast Creek Wharf**, where the fish shop is especially popular. The beer garden of the **Breakfast Creek Hotel** serves legendary steaks.

Route Notes

People who live in this area value their privacy, so do not attempt to enter any of the premises along the way unless they are noted as being open to the public.

rediscover their architectural heritage and recognise afresh the sense of building houses to suit the climate.

The next street on the left is Riverview Terrace again. Turn left here, not forgetting to look at No. 60 with its elaborate entrance stairs. Turn right into Rossiter Parade and follow it around the corner where it becomes Killara Avenue, with more lovely old houses – **Nos. 31 and 23** |10| are particularly fine.

Killara Avenue joins Windemere Road again, and on the corner to the left is **Bayuda |11|** (No. 91), the house where Sir Charles Lilley, Chief Justice and Premier of Queensland from 1868–70, lived after he retired in 1893. It had to be a very large house because Lilley, a real Victorian pater familias, fathered eight sons and five daughters. It was not usual in this period for husbands to predecease their long-suffering child-bearing wives, but Lilley left a grieving widow in 1897.

Across Windemere Road at No. 92, on the corner of Kitchener Road, is **Killara |12|**, a Federation house with Marseille tiles and a timber-gabled roof. Keep walking up Windemere Road to the end and turn left into Crescent Road where, on the other side of the street at No. 124, a fine Victorian gentleman's brick residence called Blainsleigh has huge verandahs on both storeys.

A few doors along, a Hollywood-style fantasy with two-storey portico columns and elaborately-tiled roof makes an incongruous contrast with the understated elegance of the surrounding houses, one of which is **Myrtleville, No. 100 |13|**, with its decorated verandah posts and balustrades.

Now turn left into Ludlow Street to see a large mock-Tudor house. The old workers' cottages on the corner of Ludlow Street provide an illuminating contrast to grand mansions and reflect the democratic nature of Brisbane – even the most elite suburbs contain pockets of working-class housing.

Return along Ludlow Street, and cross Crescent Road to continue down Eblin

Cooksley's House

Drive. Then turn left into Anthony Street, right into Castleton Street, and left again, crossing Hipwood Road diagonally into the very fashionable Queens Road.

All these streets contain some houses of architectural interest, if not always of heritage significance.

Walk along Queens Road where, on the right at No. 18, is **Cooksley's house |14|**. Cooksley arrived in Moreton Bay in 1858 as a penniless carpenter, but soon rose to giddy heights as Mayor of Sandgate. He built this house of brick and local sandstone, and included seven fireplaces, each of a different design.

Across the road at No. 9 is the exuberant mansion called **Palma Rosa |15|**, built of

Helidon sandstone by the celebrated Italian architect Andrea Stombuco to house his five pianos – or so the gossips of the time said. Stombuco also designed All Hallows Convent in Ann Street (see Walk No. 5).

Toorak, Brisbane style

Cross Queens Road now and go back along the other side, taking a closer look at Cooksley's house. Cross Toorak Road and veer right and uphill into Annie Street. No. 16 Annie Street is called **Toorak |16|**, the oldest and most splendid house in the district, with its three-level castellated tower, Italian marble lions and soft stone work. It was built in 1867 for the Honourable James Robert Dickson, his wife Annie and their thirteen children. (The Dicksons, but not their children, are commemorated on plaques in All Saints' Church Wickham Terrace (see Walk 3). His marble tablet on the west wall is monumental, as befits such a pillar of the community, while her much smaller one, placed in a more obscure position, says simply 'She hath done what she could'. Thirteen children is surely as much as could be expected of anyone – no wonder she died at forty-three!

The best views of Toorak are from Hillside Crescent, so turn right and follow the curve down the very steep hill. There are some important houses in this street –

notice No. 86, Toomoo, dating from 1918, which is now fronted by a new iron fence on a base of tuff stone. Lindenoa at No. 70 dates from 1908, and Eltham at No. 16 was built in 1889.

At the corner of Hillside Crescent turn left into Toorak Road and walk towards the river, noticing **No. 16, Briamon |17|**, on the right side, with outstanding examples of lovely iron lace and timber battens.

Where Toorak Road joins Kingsford Smith Drive, look for **Cameron's Rocks |18|**, the site of a Murri battleground. John Oxley came ashore here in 1824, but the memorial is a tribute to the Hamilton soldiers who fought in the First World War.

Turn right into Kingsford Smith Drive and catch a bus back into the city from stop 15, or walk along the edge of the river to Breakfast Creek, where **Newstead House |19|** on the left is Brisbane's oldest surviving house, being built in 1846. It is now a folk museum (see Opening Times) and children are always fascinated by the glass jar containing a severed finger. It belonged to an escaped convict who, when he got trapped in a wall, cut his finger off rather than risk capture and re-imprisonment.

If you need sustenance before catching the bus back into the city, cross the road at the lights and visit the **Breakfast Creek Hotel |20|**, a glorious rococo extravagance dating from 1889.

Walk key

1. War monument | 2. River bank | 3. Powerhouse | 4. Rotunda | 5. Wedding archway | 6. Avenue of old jacarandas | 7. Children's playground | 8. Kiosk | 9. Merthyr Croquet Club | 10. Coronet Flats | 11. No. 27 Hazlewood Street | 12. Santa Barbara | 13. Allawah | 14. Moreton Bay figs | 15. Briar House | 16. Holy Spirit Roman Catholic Church | 17. Wynberg

New Farm Park
Jacarandas and roses

Start

Park entrance gates at the end of Brunswick Street, opposite Oxlade Drive. City Bus 190 to the corner of Brunswick Street and Oxlade Drive, or the CityCat to New Farm.

Finish

The short walk takes place entirely inside the park and ends at the entrance gates, while the longer one takes in some of the surrounding streets with their historic buildings.

Length/Time

1.2 km/0.5 hours
3 km/1 hour

Tips

There is plenty of shade and places to sit in the park, but the longer walk calls for a hat and a water bottle.

Access

The area is quite flat, although there are savage speed humps in the ring road inside the park.

The original Murri inhabitants of this area called it Binkinba, the place of the land tortoise. White settlers were more prosaic, and when they displaced the local people and cleared the land, they gave it the most literal of names, New Farm. This was to differentiate it from the older farms in north and south Brisbane that had been established to feed the felons of the Moreton Bay penal colony from 1826–42. After free settlement began, the area was established as the Moreton Bay Jockey Club in 1846, 'a most enchanting spot, in close proximity to the river, giving the double advantage of land and water conveyance to the scene of the revelry', as it was described at the time. The race track, cricket pitches, football ovals and tennis courts have long since gone, but the original rapturous description of the area remains as true today as it was then.

Enter the park through the main gate and turn left. In 1913 the City Council purchased this site for £25,000 to be developed as a park, and it has remained one of the most popular recreational spaces in Brisbane, having more than 600,000 visitors a year.

Near a small plantation of bottle trees is a **monument |1|** to eighteen hundred Australian troops who died on the forced marches between Sandakan and Ranau, as prisoners of the Japanese.

Down by the riverside

Before you begin the walk along the ring road inside the park, wander downstream along the **river bank |2|**, where picnic tables cluster under the shade of Moreton Bay figs, hoop pines and stands of giant bamboo. From this part of the park, the views across the river are to Galloway's Hill and Hawthorne, with their odd mix of waterfront residences – the dignity of some of the older houses is in stark contrast to a pink Palatine nouveau-riche mansion of a local property developer. One of the most original houses is a charming tan-and-mustard turreted gnome's cottage straight out of Enid Blyton.

Continue along the river to the **Powerhouse |3|**, between the Humbug and Bulimba reaches of the river at Norris Point. This building used to supply the electricity for Brisbane's tramway network, and was derelict for many years, but has now been given a new burst of energy in one of the city's most brilliant transformations. The mighty ruin is now a cultural precinct for the people of Brisbane, with theatres, office and rehearsal spaces for arts companies, cafés and restaurants, picnic areas and gardens, bikeways and boardwalks, and art works reflecting both the building's technological past and the site's links with the original indigenous owners.

Walk back to the ring road inside the park and cross to the splendid **rotunda |4|**, built in 1915 and still used for free band concerts on Saturday and Sunday afternoons. (Ring the City Council's 24-hour Call Centre on 3403 8888 for details of concerts.)

Trees and flowers

It's difficult to stay on the road when the rose gardens and huge poincianas are crying out for admiration, and no officials will tell you to keep off the grass, for this is one of Brisbane's major playgrounds. Here kids of all ages show off their frisbee skills, toddlers try out their tricycles, families gather for reunions, and courting couples make the most of every opportunity.

The so-called **wedding archway |5|** of white climbing roses is understandably a drawcard for bride-and-groom photography, and the rose beds are famous for their variety as well as their extent. Many of the old-fashioned varieties are heavily scented, but don't yield to the temptation to pick them as there are always gardeners around.

There are always trees flowering in the park, with poincianas and tulip trees sharing the limelight during the summer, but the best time to go is October and early November, to see the wonderful overarching **avenue of old jacarandas |6|** in their full purple glory. This is the time of year to enjoy a picnic on the grass, with soft breezes blowing and the trees dropping their extravagance of flowers. On the other side of the jacaranda avenue is a fully equipped **children's playground |7|**, and also the toilet block.

Continue in an anti-clockwise direction, making frequent detours to smell the roses, as far as the **kiosk |8|**. Built in 1915, at the same time as the rotunda, it has recently been renovated and is no longer the dingy little ice-cream shop it used to be. The style is Edwardian rustic with overtones of colonial elegance, and you can sit inside to escape the heat, or outside in the front to watch the activity in the park.

In the weekend during croquet matches at the adjoining **Merthyr Croquet Club |9|**, the players prove the truth of Rose Macaulay's contention that croquet is a very good game for people who are annoyed with one another, giving many opportunities for venting rancour.

Past the kiosk, near the playing fields which take up most of the land on the right side of the ring road, is a dogs' lavatory bearing testimony to the importance the City Council places on public hygiene.

The walk continues full circle to the entrance gates. From here catch the bus or the CityCat back to the city, or continue for another half hour or so to see some of the fine old buildings that date back to the 1880s, and the blocks of 1930s flats so characteristic of the area.

Opening Times

The park offers pedestrian access 24 hours every day.

Refreshments

The kiosk is open Mon–Fri and public holidays 8am–4pm, Sat–Sun 7am–4pm.

Route Notes

Bicycles are allowed, and cars are subject to strict speed limits, so it is safe to walk on the ring road. There is a safe children's playground and public toilets.

As in all City Council parks, dogs on leads are allowed, but may not run free, and their owners are responsible for cleaning up after them.

Quiet back streets

Cross Brunswick Street, walking away from the river, and take the second street on the left, Elystan Road. **Coronet Flats |10|** (1930) is not just a set of brick boxes like so many buildings of the period, but has been cleverly designed to catch every breath of wind. Notice the decorative cast panels beneath the windows.

Turn left into Lower Bowen Terrace then right into Oxlade Drive, pausing to notice, at No. 42, an odd example of the architecture of the Second World War. It was built as a Naval Officers Club, but after the war was used as a public venue, and until 1960 was called the Riverside Ballroom. Many Brisbane couples retain fond memories of this building, and credit it as the place where they formed successful and long-lasting relationships. Keep following Oxlade Drive for several blocks to the junction with Hazlewood Street. On the left is one of the few remaining corner shops, Harcourt's at **No. 27 Hazlewood Street |11|**, an important link between the district's architectural past and present. Continue along Hazlewood Street until you come to Sydney Street, then turn right and proceed to the junction with Moray Street, where there are two important houses on the left.

At 209 Moray Street **Santa Barbara |12|**, with its wrought-iron grille work. This building is a fine example of the Spanish Mission style popular in the 1920s. On the opposite side, at 198–204 Moray Street, is **Allawah |13|**, built in 1890 for prominent Brisbane merchant Leopold Benjamin and

Brisbane River — Humbug Reach

one of the few remaining grand mansions in the district. Continue along Sydney Road as far as Abbott Street, then turn left past the enormous **Moreton Bay figs |14|**, some of these trees are reputed to be over a hundred years old.

From Abbott Street turn right into Merthyr Road, cross Brunswick Street and keep going for some distance to Lechmere Street, where a left turn will bring you to **Briar House |15|** at Nos. 11–15, a large house remodelled in 1888 around an earlier 1860s brick cottage. Turn left into Villiers Street, and three blocks down on the right opposite Hickey Street is the **Holy Spirit Roman Catholic Church |16|**. Its interior is even more remarkable than the exterior, a dome mural of angels and cherubs painted by William Bustard in the 1930s. Bustard, whose important stained glass windows are the pride of many other Brisbane churches, used as his models the children who lived in the area in his time, children whom he said he admired for their 'beautiful chubby innocence'. If you are particularly interested in seeing the interior telephone 3358 3744.

Villiers Street soon joins Brunswick Street; turn right here and continue as far as **Wynberg** |17|. The original cottage was built during the 1860s but, after 1890, when it became the property of railway contractor C. W. Willcocks, a number of additions gradually changed its simple integrity until it became the eclectic mixture of styles that we see today. It has been the residence of the Roman Catholic archbishops of Brisbane since 1925, when it was bought by Archbishop James Duhig.

This ends the longer New Farm walk. If you still have the energy, continue walking along Brunswick Street into the Valley, where you can wander around the shops, cafés and art galleries, and combine them with Walk 5 in this book. Otherwise, take City Bus 190 along Brunswick Street into the Valley and the CBD.

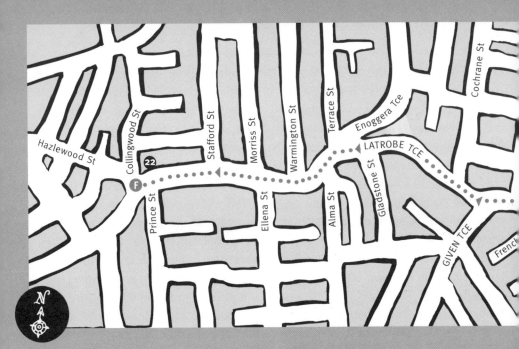

Walk key

1. Normanby Hotel | 2. Warriston |
3. Pair of terraced townhouses |
4. O'Keefe's Buildings | 5. 1880s house |
6. Striking modern house | 7. No. 63
Wellington Street | 8. Albert Villa |
9. Arts Theatre | 10. Princess Row |
11. Mysterious little house | 12. Petrie
Cottage | 13. Nos. 22 and 24 Cricket
Street | 14. Aussie Way Hostel |
15. Hotel LA | 16. Former Police
Barracks | 17. Victoria Barracks |
18. Oddfellows Hall | 19. Gambaro's
Restaurant | 20. Caxton Hotel |
21. Le Scoops | 22. Paddington
Antiques Market

Start

Bus stop 4 in Musgrave Road –
City Bus 373, 379, 380, 381 from
opposite City Hall in Adelaide Street.

Finish

Latrobe Terrace at Prince Street.
City Bus 374, 375, 382, 383, 385,
for return to the CBD.

Length/Time

4.5 km/1.5 hours

Access

This is a very hilly area, especially
the first part. This walk should not be
undertaken by people who tire easily.
The steep hills make it difficult, but not
impossible for wheelchair users.

Walk No. 12

Petrie Terrace & Paddington
Terraced treasures

The small inner-city suburb of Petrie Terrace is unique in being named after its main street. Until the 1860s the area was known only as Ti Tree Flats, and its address was 'back of the gaol', built on the street called Petrie Terrace after the stonemason Andrew Petrie. (To avoid confusion, the suburb will now be referred to as Petrie Terrace and the street as Petrie Terrace.) In the 1980s a City Council bent on 'progress' built a ring road right through the suburb, which has spoiled the character of Hale Street. Petrie Terrace itself has retained its charm, and still gives some idea of what Petrie-Terrace might have been like around the turn of the century.

From bus stop 4 in Musgrave Road, walk a few metres back towards the city, noticing the flamboyant **Normanby Hotel |1|** (1890) on the other side of the road. On the right, at No. 6–8 Musgrave Road, is **Warriston |2|**, which has had quite a chequered history. Since it was built in 1886 it has been a domestic residence, a boarding house, a private school and commercial offices, and now its future seems uncertain.

The old and the new

Walk past the carpet and bicycle shops on the corner of the Normanby Fiveways and turn right into Petrie Terrace, where an identical **pair of terraced townhouses |3|** give no indication that they were, in fact, built more than a century apart. Florence House, built in 1877, is the older, but it is difficult to spot the differences.

Petrie Terrace contains more terrace houses than the rest of Brisbane combined, and the two across Mountjoy Street, once known as **O'Keefe's Buildings |4|**, date from 1881. Today they both operate as popular function centres, with wedding receptions and busloads of tourists being their main source of income. Some people think they have been restored with more exuberance than good taste, but the tourists keep on coming.

From Mountjoy Street turn left and then right into St James Street. On a wedge-shaped block where this meets Rutland Street an **1880s house |5|** has been restored, with the fibro verandah fill-ins replaced with open timber battens. At the end of St James Street is a **striking modern house |6|**, looking more at home with its older neighbours than one might have thought, and from here you can see the backs of Florence House and its neighbour taking up the whole allotment from Petrie Terrace to St James Street.

Return to Mountjoy Street and cross into Terrace Street for an unusual view of Princess Row, which will be seen later from a different angle. Take the first right into the narrow shady Wellington Lane, with its small blocks of units which reproduce quite successfully the architectural idiom of the area. From here there are commanding views across to the east.

At the foot of the lane turn left into Lutwyche Street, and then left again into Wellington Street, which runs uphill to meet Petrie Terrace again. On the left-hand side of **Wellington Street at No. 63 |7|** is a remarkable little two-storey house with an overhanging verandah, one of the few remaining examples of a shop-house, where the shopkeeper's family lived upstairs.

To the right behind a huge old weeping fig tree is No. 42, much in need of care, and a sad contrast to its neighbours at Nos. 38 and 34, both of which have been gentrified in different styles. Higher up at No. 23 on the left are four old attached houses with dormer windows, each roof higher than the other as they climb up the hillside and, on the corner of Ormonde Street, the stately old **Albert Villa |8|** (1886) which is also undergoing renovation.

At the top of the hill turn right into Petrie Terrace. Pass Romeo's Restaurant, serving some of the best Italian food in Brisbane, but open only at night, and then the **Arts Theatre |9|**, home of Brisbane's oldest amateur theatrical company.

Near the Arts Theatre is **Princess Row |10|**, very dilapidated now, but still mostly used for residential purposes, and outstanding because of the dormer windows and sandstone footings. Built in 1863, these are among the oldest buildings in the street.

Up and down the side streets

There is a pattern to this walk, which entails going down all the side streets and returning to Petrie Terrace. Turn next into Princess Street and take the first right into Ormonde Street and then left into Crown Street, where there is a great variety of workers' cottages and larger houses in various states of repair and disrepair. Most of them take up the full block and are built very close to the footpath – gardens were an unnecessary luxury for the hard-working people who first built here, but later residents, more concerned with privacy, have filled in the verandahs with lattice screening.

Turn right from Crown Street into Princess Street again, and follow it down to the corner of Hale Street, where there is a **mysterious little house |11|** reputed to have once been a mortuary for the Hale Street cemetery, and converted to a residential dwelling when the cemetery closed down in 1875. It may be the cross-shaped structure of the building which gave rise to

Opening Times

The **Military Museum** in the Victoria Barracks in Petrie Terrace (3233 4011 for opening times). Shops and eating places are open at the usual hours.

Refreshments

The main café strip is along Caxton Street. Petrie Terrace and the surrounding streets are mainly residential, but there is always the Normanby Hotel at the very beginning of the walk.

Route Notes

The City Council Heritage Trail booklet has good information on the history of Paddington. It is obtainable from any Brisbane City Council Customer Service Centre. The only public toilets in this area are in the cafés and hotels.

this assumption, for there are no records existing to confirm it.

On the way back up Princess Street, notice **Petrie Cottage |12|** (1878) on the corner of Crown Street, then a pretty blue cottage and finally, at No. 59, another shop-house dating from 1878, in good condition and obviously well loved and cared for.

Turn right again into Petrie Terrace, go past Pratten Street and turn right into Cricket Street. Here, at **Nos. 22 and 24 |13|**, a worker's cottage like a doll's house stands side-by-side with a middle-class house of the 1880s, bought in 1887 by a Brisbane widow, Mrs Anna Dyne.

Further down is the **Aussie Way Hostel |14|**, in a beautifully restored two-storey house with iron lace on both upper and lower verandahs.

Almost at the end of Cricket Street, turn left at a sharp angle into Menzies Street and walk up the hill again, where Chase's House (No. 30) has splendid finials at the end of the gabled roof and an ornate verandah. Then turn right once more and follow Petrie Terrace to the corner of Caxton Street, where the modernised **Hotel LA |15|** disguises its 1887 origins very effectively.

Police and the military

Across the road is the three-storey brick building of the former **Police Barracks |16|**, built on the site of the Brisbane Gaol. The trapdoor used for executions at eight o'clock on Monday mornings was removed only in 1939, a relic of a grisly history that is probably unknown to the rowdy young

A former shop-house

people who enjoy the building's new life as a lively nightclub.

To the left of the Police Barracks, the stately **Victoria Barracks |17|**, built in 1864, was the second structure erected on Petrie Terrace, or Green Hill as it was then called. The beauty of its original lines has been desecrated with modern additions, but it is still an important monument to the military history of Queensland. The military museum is open to the public (3233 4011 for opening times).

Turn right into Caxton Street, walking along the left side to see the facades of the old buildings across the road. The original inhabitants of the **Oddfellows Hall |18|** on the corner of Cathie Street have long since passed on, but their building still retains its distinctive decorated façade, with particularly fine ornamentation along the top. The tenants of this row of buildings now include a bespoke tailor who has been there for years, a body-piercing specialist, and various cafés and restaurants. The Italianate building with its fake statuary is **Gambaro's Restaurant |19|**, celebrated for its seafood rather than its décor.

On the left are a number of eating houses, including Gambaro's other establishment, a takeaway fish shop justly renowned for Queensland's famous mud crabs and other shellfish, guaranteed to be always fresh. The pub just past Gambaro's takeaway is the **Caxton Hotel |20|**.

When you get to the lights at Hale Street, look left to see the famous Lang Park football ground, built on the site of the old cemetery. Caxton Street itself is said to run through the old Jewish section of the cemetery.

Past the traffic lights Caxton Street becomes Given Terrace, the centre of the suburb of Paddington, a lively and increasingly gentrified suburb which still retains much of its original gypsy charm.

Serious shopping

On the left, notice the houses built above a high wall to escape the noise and fumes of the traffic. Next comes the Paddo Tavern, and past Guthrie Street the fascinating row of funky shops and eating houses begins – second-hand clothes, exotic delicatessens, furniture shops, knick-knack emporia, bathroom supplies, bookshops, bridal wear, interior design. It's a wonderful stretch for shopping and browsing, and the cafés are all fun. **Le Scoops |21|**, on the corner of Hayward Street, makes a large range of superb ice-creams.

Given Terrace becomes Latrobe Terrace, where you could spend all day browsing, eating and appreciating many fine old buildings (the City Council Heritage Trail, Series 10, Latrobe and Given Terraces, will give you all the historical detail you need). Past the Enoggera Terrace intersection is the **Paddington Antiques Market |22|**, an old picture theatre now used by various small second-hand dealers, where you may pick up a bargain.

Here the walk ends. The bus back to the city stops opposite Prince Street.

Walk key

1. Normanby Hotel | 2. Old stone wall | 3. Albert Park | 4. Brisbane Grammar School | 5. Brisbane Girls' Grammar School | 6. Victoria Park | 7. Victoria Park Golf Course | 8. Royal Brisbane Hospital | 9. St Joseph's College | 10. Centenary Aquatic Centre | 11. Queensland Museum | 12. Victoria Terraces | 13. No. 383 Gregory Terrace, Eaton | 14. Brisbane Central School | 15. Hipwood Street | 16. Ancient mango trees | 17. Home of Inner Beauty

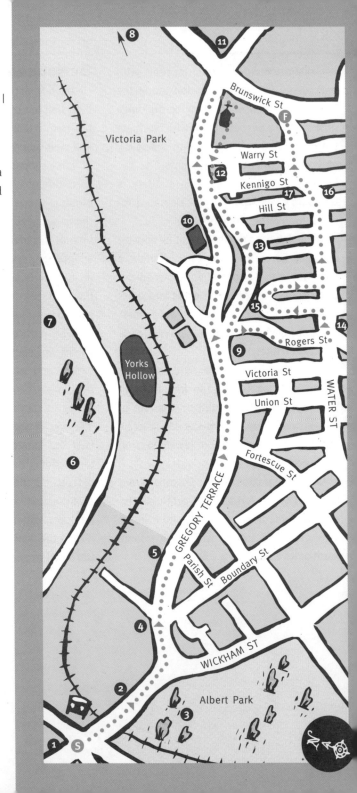

Gregory Terrace
Classical elegance

Start

Normanby Hotel, Normanby
Fiveways. Bus stop 4 in
Musgrave Road – City Bus 373,
379, 380, 381 from opposite
City Hall in Adelaide Street.

Finish

Brunswick Street, Fortitude
Valley. City Bus 334, 360, 361,
364, 370, 374, 375, 379.

Length/Time

3.5 km/1.25 hours

Access

Some gentle hills in the side
streets off Gregory Terrace.
Wheelchair users may choose to
avoid the steeper side streets.

As Brisbane Town expanded, the
wealthier settlers moved onto the
ridges around it, to take advantage
of the splendid view and the cooling
summer breezes. But the early settlers
also appreciated open spaces, and a
walk along Gregory Terrace in Spring
Hill shows how, even close to the city,
large areas of parklands escaped the
chainsaws of the developers. Terrace
houses, which have always been a
feature of Melbourne and Sydney
domestic architecture, have never
been particularly popular in Brisbane,
where houses were built to catch every
breath of wind, but the late 20th century
saw a renewed interest in this type
of architecture, and there are some
impressive blocks of new terraces.

The Normanby Fiveways is one of the busiest intersections in Brisbane. From the bus stop in Musgrave Road, cross with care to the **Normanby Hotel |1|**, a flamboyant structure built around 1890 to catch the passing trade from the city out to the western suburbs. The old fig trees by the hotel have managed to survive the depredations of the traffic and the best efforts of developers and town planners alike, to the extent that no city council would now dare to suggest their removal.

The school route

From the hotel, cross the railway bridge in College Road, walking past an **old stone wall |2|** from the 19th century. Across the road on the right is the beginning of the vast expanse of **Albert Park |3|**, with sweeping views of the city. College Road soon joins Gregory Terrace, so turn left here, past **Brisbane Grammar School |4|**, one of Queensland's most prestigious boys' private schools.

Opened in Roma Street in 1869 with ninety-four students and four masters, it moved to its present site in 1881 when the neo-gothic Great Hall and classrooms were built. The school, which has a very high academic standard, now has 1200 students.

A little further along are the gracious but less formal buildings of the **Brisbane Girls' Grammar School |5|**, with a fine arched front and a low cream paling fence. The main building, designed by architect Richard Gailey, was opened in 1884 when the school separated from the Boys' Grammar School, moved from Wickham Terrace and became an institution in its own right. The school still shares with its brother school the motto, 'nil sine labore', or 'nothing without work'.

Across the road, on your right, No. 109 is an authentic old colonial house almost hidden behind the palms that are a feature of this street, and there is a quaint white worker's cottage next door.

Just past Girls' Grammar are the broad slopes of **Victoria Park |6|**, built on 68 hectares of land transferred to the Brisbane Council in 1896.

Leave the footpath if you wish and wander at your leisure beneath giant Moreton Bay figs, and catch a view of the **Victoria Park Golf Course |7|** (very handy for medicos between their ward rounds), the **Royal Brisbane Hospital |8|** and the northern suburbs. The park would be perfect were it not for the interruptions of the railway tracks that run through it.

Gregory Terrace was once a prime area for boarding houses (although most of them have gone down in the world now), and across the road No. 183, Rutland Court, is a typical stucco edifice of the 1930s. Next door Tyler Terrace looks like a renovated 19th century block, but is in fact modern, having been built in 1988 when the street was smartened up. There are more modern terraces past Fortescue Street.

Further along, just past the Victoria Street corner, is an old building made of local pink porphyry with wooden extensions on the back, part of another of the exclusive group of private schools in this area. **St Joseph's College |9|** is run by the Christian Brothers, and the ecclesiastical windows of this building leave you in no doubt as to its allegiance.

The school, known more familiarly by Brisbane people as Terrace, moved here in 1875 from its original site in the Pugin Chapel in the grounds of St Stephen's Cathedral (see Walk No. 1), onto land donated by a Christian Brothers Old Boy in Ireland. The first single-storey building was completed in 1879, and an extra wing and a second storey added eight years later to complete what is now known as College Hall.

Stay on the left, and at the traffic lights swing into a loop that cuts into Victoria Park. The road offers even better views to the northern suburbs, and the road leads to the **Centenary Aquatic Centre |10|**, recently refurbished to bring it up to world standard.

The old museum
The road slopes downhill at this point, towards Bowen Bridge Road, but instead of keeping to the footpath wander through the gardens in the median strip for a better view of the buildings on the other side of the road. At the traffic lights at the end of Gregory Terrace, look across at the great brick and stone folly that was once the **Queensland Museum |11|**, a Victorian masterpiece or monstrosity according to your aesthetic taste. Vacated by the Museum when the Cultural Centre was built on South Bank, it is badly in need of repair

Refreshments
Apart from the Normanby Hotel at the beginning of the walk, there are no refreshment stops until you reach a corner store near the end.

Route Notes
There are no public toilets along this route.

and is not usually open to the public. There is probably no need to cross the road to investigate it – it isn't open to the public, and looks much better from a distance.

Cross to the other side of Gregory Terrace now and retrace your steps, noticing the very good iron lace on the verandah of No. 451, which used to be a Carmelite monastery; the barley-twist columns on the stucco house called Carrington at No. 445 (on the corner of Warry Street); and the modern **Victoria Terraces |12|** on the corner of Kennigo Street.

Where the road divides at Kennigo Street, take the left fork and walk past a block of modern brick and timber units on the corner of Hill Street, an example of colonial reproduction that works marvellously; then pass a motel at No. 397, and Dunvegan at No. 391, a fine example of a 1930s rooming house that, rarely in this part of Brisbane, has not gone to seed.

Eaton, No. 383 |13|, a beautifully preserved (as opposed to restored) colonial bungalow with a good roof line and huge verandahs, takes up the whole block between Park and Kinross Streets, while across Kinross Street is Cussane, an unrestored wooden cottage from the 1920s with an atypical tiled roof.

Turn left into Rogers Street at the traffic lights for an unsurpassed view of the city skyline and St Paul's Church on St Paul's Terrace, then wander down the steep hill, where the eclectic architecture of St Joseph's dominates on the right. Notice especially the way traditional pink

Old Queensland Museum

porphyry stone is still being used in modern buildings, and the lovely mix of old workers' cottages on the right, not all of which have been gentrified.

Colonial cottages

Turn left into Water Street and notice, across the road in the grounds of the **Brisbane Central School |14|,** a number of impressive poinciana trees. Turn left again into **Hipwood Street |15|,** which forms a loop with Royal Avenue. This pretty enclave contains a wide variety of cottages, in all stages of repair and restoration, as well as a much larger timber house, No. 17 Royal Avenue, on the left.

Royal Avenue comes out at Water Street. Continue away from the city, past the RACQ depot, and cross Quarry Street. On the left side of the street are some high-set houses from the 1930s, interspersed with a few modern cottages, and on the right, up Greiner Street, some **ancient mango trees** |16|. There's also a convenience store on the corner where you can buy cold drinks.

One of the loveliest houses in Brisbane is just across the road on the corner of Kennigo Street, an eccentric little two-storey fantasy that has unfortunately been converted from a domestic residence into a New Age soul palace called the **Home of Inner Beauty** |17|.

Leaving such temptations aside, walk to where Water Street joins the frantic rush of Brunswick Street. Cross the road carefully to catch a bus back to the city.

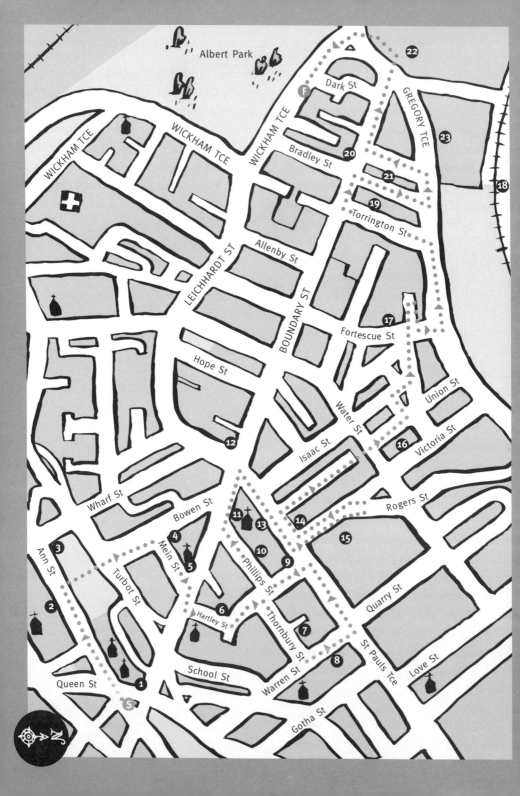

Spring Hill

Workers' paradise

Start

Orient Hotel, corner of Queen and Ann Streets. City Bus 300, 306, 322, 370, 375, 379 all from Adelaide Street.

Finish

St Andrew's Hospital, Wickham Terrace. City Bus 372, 373, 23

Length/Time

About 3.5 km/1.25 hours 7 km if combined with Walk No. 13 along Gregory Terrace.

Tips

Because of the hills and the heat, it is not advisable to take this walk in the middle of the day. The steep hills are difficult for wheelchairs.

The first houses in Spring Hill were built in the late 1850s, mostly two-roomed shingle-clad workers' cottages. By the turn of the century the working-class suburb had acquired a tough reputation, and a common derogatory phrase of the 1920s was 'he looks like a Spring Hill thug'. But now gentrification has taken over, and the tiny workers' cottages are eagerly sought after by business couples. Still, a walk through Spring Hill presents a unique microcosm of the city, as planning regulations stipulate all new buildings must be in character with the suburb.

Walk key

1. Orient Hotel | 2. St John's Anglican Cathedral | 3. Cathedral Square | 4. Old worker's cottage | 5. Spiritualist Church | 6. No. 20 Hartley Street | 7. No. 26 Thornbury Street | 8. Villa Maria Hostel and Nursing Home | 9. Artist's house | 10. Dahrl Court | 11. Dolls' house | 12. Alliance Hotel | 13. Presbyterian Church | 14. Interior decorator's shop | 15. Brisbane Central School | 16. 'Spring Hill Vernacular' | 17. Nos. 134–38 Fortescue Street | 18. Victoria Park | 19. Spring Hill Baths | 20. As You Like It on Spring Hill | 21. Nos. 82–98 Bradley Street | 22. Brisbane Boys' Grammar School | 23. Brisbane Girls' Grammar School

The walk starts at the **Orient Hotel** |1|, on the corner of Queen and Ann Streets. Walk along Ann Street towards the CBD, passing **St John's Anglican Cathedral** |2| on the left. At the corner with Wharf Street is **Cathedral Square** |3|, a tranquil shaded park with a coffee shop on the plaza. Walk through this square to Turbot Street and, from the other side of the road, take Bowen Street to the left, then turn right into Mein Street. On the corner is an **old tumbledown worker's cottage** |4| with lattice over the verandah, in striking contrast to the modern low-rise apartment blocks at Nos. 37 and 33.

Then comes a renovation at No. 29, next to a new Spring Hill style house at No. 25, and a very old house, partly overgrown with ivy, at No. 21.

Boundary Street

Mein Street comes out into Boundary Street where, on the corner, the typically 1960s red brick **Spiritualist Church** |5| still dispenses an odd mixture of worship and communication with people on 'the other side' every Sunday at 2.30pm and 7pm.

Boundary Street acquired its very pedestrian name from its function, for until 1859 it marked the boundary of the town limits beyond which Murri people were not allowed to come, a prohibition which lasted well into the 20th century. The first houses, built in the late 1850s, were mostly tiny workers' cottages with gables, verandahs at the front and lean-tos at the back. Cross Boundary Street with care, and walk up Hartley Street, just below the Ambulance Service. **No. 20** |6|, on the left, an old house almost obscured behind greenery, used to be a Mecca for painters in the 1960s when Jon Molvig painted and taught there. Other important figures in the art world like Robert Hughes, Charles Blackman, John Perceval, Ann Thomson and Hugh Sawrey dropped in occasionally to join in post-class carousing, but these days it leads a more sedate existence as a rooming house.

Turn left again into Gloucester Street, past some pretty cottages, then right into Thornbury Street, where at **No. 26** |7|, perched above a wall, is a beautiful old town house, an example of how such buildings can be restored without losing their special character.

From Thornbury turn left into Warren Street where, immediately opposite, you will see the imposing red brick bulk of **Villa Maria Hostel and Nursing Home** |8|, where the Sisters of the Perpetual Adoration look after the frail elderly.

Around St Paul's Terrace

Follow the steep climb of Warren Street to St Paul's Terrace and turn left. Through the cutting on the left is No. 111, a very early house that makes one long to see it restored to its original state.

The next street on the left is Gloucester again, on the corner of which is an **artist's house** |9|, painted in what can only be called courageous colours. On the way down Gloucester Street, notice a very unusual house for Brisbane, made of the local stone known as tuff, and the two-storey building at No. 23 with a fine overhanging verandah.

Turn right into Philips Street, where **Dahrl Court |10|** on the left is the sole 1920s building among all the modern apartment blocks in the street, and then right again into Boundary Street, where the splendid **two-storey dolls' house |11|** at No. 283 still boasts its original timber and tin. It nestles incongruously next to The Players' Inn, a much more modern establishment in every way, which advertises itself as 'A Gentleman's Playground'.

At the next large intersection, with Leichhardt Street to the left and St Paul's Terrace to the right, look down Boundary Street for a fine view of the Story Bridge. Across the road, on the corner of Leichhardt and Boundary, is one of the few remaining grand hotels that used to grace the area. **The Alliance |12|** was built in 1888 in the then-fashionable Renaissance style, but she lost much of her former elegance when her iron lace verandahs were pulled down. The old lady's bone structure is still good, however, in spite of her raddled appearance.

Rather than crossing over to the hotel, cross Boundary Street to the right at the lights and proceed along St Paul's Terrace. Half a block along is the lovely St Paul's **Presbyterian Church |13|** (see Opening Times) after which the street was named. The Sabbath School Hall (1886) and the church (1889) are both listed by the National Trust of Queensland. Many people decry the 1990s fashion of erecting build-

Opening Times

St Paul's Church: Tue 10am–2pm

Refreshments

There is a café in Cathedral Square at the start of the walk, and a coffee shop in St Paul's Terrace near the corner of Rogers Street. The Alliance Hotel is open during normal pub hours.

ings with reflecting glass walls, but the office block next but one to the church is a rare exception, reflecting the church and spire as in a fairy-tale mirror.

Cross St Paul's Terrace to see Vailima, an old block of flats in Tudor revival style, and walk on to turn left into Rogers Street. The premises on the corner (1863) have had a colourful history, being at various times a hansom cab depot, a corner store, an infamous brothel and now, more respectably, an **interior decorator's shop** |14|.

Most of the cottages in Rogers Street have been very carefully restored, and the huge old shade trees lining the road and the playgrounds of the **Brisbane Central School** |15| on the other side make it doubly attractive. Traffic calming has been introduced in this street, so there are few cars to distract you as you look at No. 26, with its lace and fretwork trim, and the iron lace verandahs on the houses below it.

Return to St Paul's Terrace and turn right, walking towards the city. Mrs Dibble's Deli, a modern building which captures all the flavour of shops of a hundred years ago, serves good coffee and cold drinks. Just before Union Street, at No. 54, is an interesting example of an old factory recycled to a new existence as a luxury town house. In spite of all the modernisation, however, the galvanised iron at the back is original.

Wander down Union Street, where there are more old or renovated cottages and, when the road comes to a dead end, cross the strip of vegetation and Water Street to reach the other part of Union Street.

No. 283 Boundary Street

Colonial cottages, old and new

Continue up Union Street, and on the right is a house in the **'Spring Hill Vernacular'** |16|, a good example of how modern architects are designing buildings which blend in with older ones.

On the top corner of Elcot Lane, on the left, is one of the original houses of the area, dilapidated, totally unrestored, but still inhabited. The width of the horizontal weatherboards marks it out as being very early, probably from the 1880s.

Walk to the end of Elcot Lane and turn right into Isaac Street to reach the junction with York Street. On the corner here, an old corner store has been converted into a residential dwelling, another of the many forms of building transformation in this area.

Turn left into York Street, which ends in a T-junction with Fortescue Street. Across the road at **Nos. 134–38 Fortescue Street** |17| is a group of very pretty cottages. Turn right into Fortescue Street, and just before it meets Gregory Terrace turn into the dead-end Reading Street, where cottages on half-size blocks blend happily with modern units in a peaceful inner-city haven only metres away from major traffic routes.

Straight ahead as you come out of Fortescue Street into Gregory Terrace is the huge expanse of **Victoria Park** |18|. Don't cross Gregory Terrace, but turn left, walking past buildings old and new, trendy and sleazy, all rubbing along cheerfully side by side.

Turn left into Torrington Street, where the old **Spring Hill Baths** |19| (1886), seemingly unchanged since they were first built, are still very popular, in spite of the smart new Centenary Aquatic Centre further along Gregory Terrace.

At the end of Torrington Street, turn right into Boundary Street again, noticing the restaurant **As You Like It on Spring Hill** |20| in a pleasant old building across the road. Continue up Boundary Street to the next block, and turn right into Bradley Street. There are some wonderful old cottages

here, especially Nos. 103 and 107 on the right, and on the left a group built right out over the footpath **Nos. 82–98** |21|.

At the end of Bradley Street turn left again into Gregory Terrace, and almost immediately left again into Parish Street. This street takes you back to Boundary Street, and has numerous examples of tiny cottages on the equally tiny building blocks that were considered suitable for workers in the 19th century. No. 18 has a special charm, as have Nos. 27–37.

Turn right again into Boundary Street, and walk up the hill to the traffic lights. On the way there is a very different view, the backs of the seedy boarding houses on Gregory Terrace, still occupied by pensioners and down-and-outs of all ages, a reminder of the time when this was the main place to rent a cheap room in the city.

Where Boundary Street meets Gregory Terrace, **Brisbane Boys' Grammar School** |22| is the dominant architectural feature, with **Brisbane Girls' Grammar School** |23| immediately to its right.

Turn left, and walk along Wickham Terrace. Catch a bus from the corner of Dark Street back to the city or, for a longer walk, follow Walk 13 (Gregory Terrace).

Walk key

1. Chelmer Railway Station |
2. No. 10 Lama Street, Dalmuir | 3. Iron lacework |
4. Mango trees |
5. No. 148 Laurel Avenue |
6. Steep river bank |
7. Flowering trees |
8. Modern house |
9. Floraville | 10. The Laurels | 11. Queensland Police College |
12. Indooroopilly Bridge |
13. Indooroopilly Railway Station

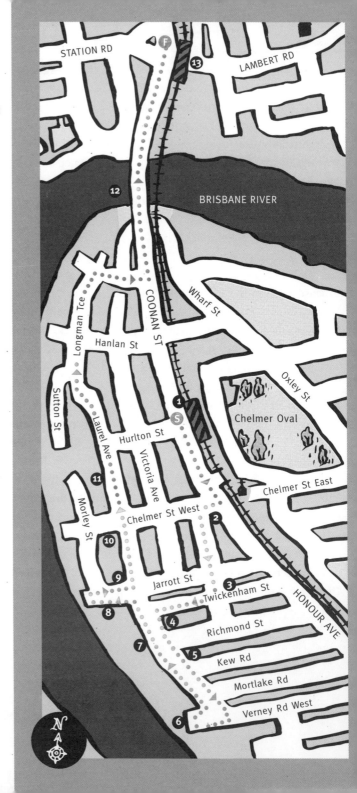

Chelmer

Gracious living

Start

Honour Avenue at Chelmer Railway Station. City Train from Roma Street or Central Station (Ipswich line).

Finish

Indooroopilly Railway Station (Ipswich line).

Length/Time

4.7 km/1.75 hours

Tips

Easy walking, mostly level, with many shady areas.

Access

Not all kerbs have wheelchair ramp.

The quiet riverside suburb of Chelmer is one of Brisbane's hidden secrets. For those who appreciate domestic architecture, its broad leafy streets provide some of the finest examples of the 19th century houses known popularly as 'colonials', and the later 20th century 'Queenslanders', some renovated even beyond their original glory, and some almost in their original state. A lovely stretch of the river provides uninterrupted views of the Walter Taylor or Indooroopilly Bridge, which marks the height of the 1974 floods. There is still great demand for the tiny flats in the pylons at each end of the bridge, but the lucky residents prefer to stay put, so that vacancies occur only rarely.

Take the Honour Avenue exit from the **Chelmer Railway Station** |1| and turn left, then take the second right into Chelmer Street West and go left into Lama Street. There are a number of fine old examples of colonial architecture in this street, like **Dalmuir at No. 10** |2|.

Opposite, behind a huge weeping fig, is another house which is perhaps more typical of the era. Notice the quaint porch with elaborate detail at No. 16, and the characteristic timber decorations on the verandah of No. 27. No. 29 has a rare hexagonal sunroom, while the latticework sunscreen on the verandah of No. 34 is characteristic of this period.

Iron lace and mango trees

Cross over Jarrott Street into Little Lama Street, where there is a particularly fine example of **iron lace work** |3| on the first house on the left.

Turn right into Twickenham Street, where the houses on the left display an eclectic selection of verandah styles. On the corner of Twickenham Street and Laurel Avenue, on the left note the diagonal timber verandah railings and **the huge mango trees** |4|.

One of the most powerful memories of a Brisbane childhood summer is the scent of mangoes rotting in the gutters, the fruit being too stringy even for Australia's famous mango chutney.

Turn left into Laurel Avenue. There's a good mix of historical examples here – the very old house at **No. 148** |5| on the left side of the street has an unusual tongue-and-groove verandah ceiling and wide verandah steps which identify it as being from the late 19th century.

At No. 160, on the corner of Richmond Street, the famous 'under-the-house' area which provided cooling in hot weather and a place for children to play and clothes to dry in the wet season has been filled in with brick to create extra rooms, while the stucco and brick exterior of No. 168 is a rare example of 1930s architecture.

Crossing Kew Road, continue to the corner of Verney Road West, where there is a splendid example of a sensitively restored old colonial. For a glimpse of the Brisbane River, turn right into Verney Road West and wander to the end, where the **steep river bank** |6| is a virtual jungle of blue gums, camphor laurels and small palms. The houses here went under during the great floods of 1974.

Return to Laurel Avenue and retrace your steps with the river on your left, to see some fine old specimens of **flowering trees** |7| which are one of the glories of Brisbane. They provide colour and variety practically all year round, and more than compensate for the scarcity of flowering annuals in suburban gardens.

The poinciana trees at No.85 are in full bloom in December, while the jacarandas at No. 179 precede them by six weeks or so, and remind students that end-of-year examinations are drawing near. Continue past a grove of rainforest trees including palms and hoop pines at No. 143, to more camphor laurels at No. 127.

River views

Turn left into Jarrott Street for another glimpse of the river. On the left is a stand of hoop pines forming a backdrop to the **very modern house |8|** at No. 88. These trees lined the river bank before white settlement. Across the river at Fig Tree Pocket, low-set houses nestle into the bush on the steep banks, and if you listen carefully you may hear whip birds and currawongs. Look left into Morley Street for an example of how the huge estates on Laurel Avenue, which used to go right down to the river, have now been subdivided for newer, smaller houses.

Return to Laurel Avenue and turn left, noticing **Floraville |9|** at No. 115, another example of sensitive restoration, with particularly impressive verandahs. No. 103 has a shady tangled garden and a front gable with rare timber detailing at the apex, while **The Laurels |10|** (No. 89) boasts one of the few iron fences in this area. The Laurels also has a double chimney stack, another rarity, a roof top with iron lacework ridge cap and finials, and large doors and French windows.

Cross Chelmer Street West and continue along Laurel Avenue, where on both sides of the street are some of the best old colonial houses. Particularly noteworthy are the low-set No. 67; the entrance stairs at No. 60; the tiled roof of Onkaparinga at No. 43; the elegant lines of No. 35; and a group of modern houses from Nos. 32 to 36.

Refreshments

This is a quiet residential area, and there are no shops on this walk until the end, where there are coffee bars, takeaways and a hotel opposite Indooroopilly Railway Station.

Fantasy land

No. 17, now the **Queensland Police College |11|**, is notable for its ancient fig trees, and No. 7 is a real old hybrid, a Gone-with-the-Wind kind of house, with iron lace, caryatids, fountains and a sandstone front fence.

The road takes a dog-leg at this point and becomes Longman Terrace. As you cross Hanlan Street look right and left for many pleasant low-set houses – Nos. 93, 73 and 48 are outstanding.

Turn right into Regatta Street, continue until you come to Honour Avenue, turn left and walk across the Walter Taylor Bridge, commonly called **Indooroopilly Bridge |12|**, where people still live in the apartments in the pylons at each end. From the bridge there are excellent views of the Chelmer reach of the Brisbane River.

Return to the city by train from **Indooroopilly Railway Station |13|**.

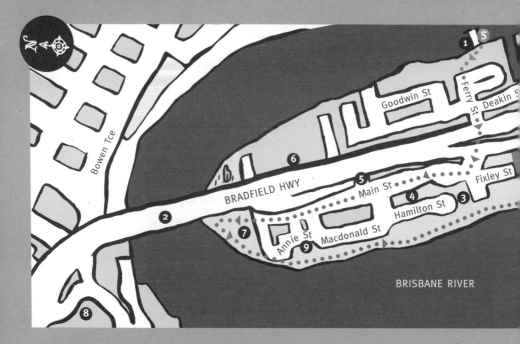

BRISBANE RIVER

Walk key

1. Dockside terminal | 2. Story Bridge | 3. Old lock-up and police residence | 4. Silverwells | 5. Story Bridge Hotel | 6. Yungaba | 7. Captain John Burke Park | 8. All Hallows School | 9. James Warner Park | 10. St Mary's Anglican Church | 11. River Plaza cross-river ferry

Start

Dockside ferry terminal – from the CBD, catch the cross-river ferry at the Riverside terminal. Note that the CityCat does not stop here.

Finish

The shorter walk finishes at the Thornton Street ferry terminal, while the longer walk continues under the Captain Cook Bridge to the River Plaza ferry terminal, to catch a cross-river ferry back to the CBD.

Length/Time

2 km/0.75 hours or 3.5 km/1.25 hours
This walk can be combined with the South Bank Parklands Walk No. 4.

Access

Steep steps lead down to the river bank and are not suitable for people with mobility difficulties.

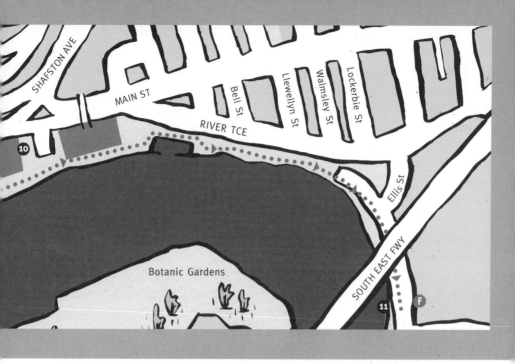

Walk No. 16

Kangaroo Point
Cliffs and colonial charm

Kangaroo Point began as a prestigious residential area, safely isolated across the river from the commercial bustle of Brisbane Town, but when the Brisbane River began to be heavily dredged in the 1880s, large ships started to come up the river, and wharves soon lined the south bank from the Kangaroo Point cliffs to the Victoria Bridge. Industrial enterprises moved in, and the area lost its status as a desirable suburb. But when the Evans Deakin shipyards closed down in 1976 the area became gentrified again, and is now a fine example of a suburb that is being restored to its original grandeur. This walk takes in some of the area's colourful history, including some of the lovely homes of the first settlers in the late 1850s and 1860s.

Alight from the ferry at the **Dockside terminal** |1|, walk up and turn right into the pleasant riverside residential and commercial development of that name, formerly the site of major shipyards but now one of the south side's most desirable addresses. Wander through the gentle landscaping with its canals and wooden bridges, past the shops and the Snug Harbour café, and eventually come out into Ferry Street.

At the end of Ferry Street turn right into Deakin Street, which runs parallel with and below the beginning of the Bradfield Highway over the massive **Story Bridge** |2|, which was opened in 1940. It was named after the engineer J. D. Story, who had designed the Sydney Harbour Bridge, and building began with a tower on each bank of the river, from which construction extended across the river and eventually joined in the middle. An elderly nun in All Hallows Convent tells the story of being a young novice during the war with a view of the bridge from her cell window, and the thrill of wondering whether the two sides would actually join up.

The road across the bridge is the Bradfield Highway, named for the bridge's modest designer. An underpass takes you to the other side of the bridge and into Main Street, where you turn right.

Houses of the 1860s

Some of the district's oldest houses, dating back to the 1860s, are still standing in this street. At the corner of Main and Thornton Streets is the **old lock-up and police residence** |3|, parts of which belong to the original building of 1872.

The Brisbane City Council Heritage booklet notes that the lock-up was built in response to a request from the local constable who, a full fifteen years before the Kangaroo Point Hotel was erected, did not have 'a secure building in which to lodge drunkards'. John Petrie built the original lock-up, and its cell doors are part of the present building, which dates from 1910. Behind this building is the former residence of the water police (early 1870s), which was relocated here in 1901 from its original site in the Botanic Gardens.

Silverwells |4| (261–7 Main Street) is the oldest surviving home in Kangaroo Point. Built in the early 1860s, it seems to be made of stone, but is actually two brick buildings joined together and cement-rendered to suggest the more prestigious building material.

No. 255 Main Street, dating back only to 1890, is a charming example of a low-set colonial house.

Pubs, hostels and migrants

On the corner of Baildon Street is the **Story Bridge Hotel** |5|, formerly the Kangaroo Point Hotel, (1886). Until the closing of the shipyards in 1976 it was a basic painters-and-dockers pub without much finesse, but after the shipyard workers drifted away the pub's clientele changed.

Between 1988 and 1992 it was primarily a backpackers establishment, but in the last few years it has been sympathetically restored and its distinctive lace verandahs reinstated, so that it is now close to its original glory and one of the prettiest heritage hotels in town.

The impressive front view of the pub shows the three storeys newly painted in deep ox-blood, with the splendid iron lace and wooden verandahs picked out in white. Inside, the 1950s dining room has been spruced up with mustard paint (where would we be without heritage colours?), polished wood and some cheerful leadlighting over the bar, and the walls are hung with old metal advertising signs. Behind the pub proper is the famous Bomb Shelter, which has live entertainment six nights a week, with cool and hot jazz on Sunday afternoons.

At 120 Main Street is the entrance to **Yungaba |6|**, built in 1887 as a hostel for newly arrived migrants. This is still one of its many functions, but it has had other occupants, too – hungry people seeking food handouts during the economic depressions of the 1890s and 1930s, mental patients en route to the Dunwich Benevolent Asylum on Stradbroke Island, and returning soldiers, able-bodied as well as wounded, after the Boer War and the First and Second World Wars. After the privations of European winters, the migrants who were housed there from 1947 probably appreciated its name, which means Land of the Sun.

The building has recently been heritage listed by the National Trust of Queensland, and is now used as a conference and

Opening Times
Story Bridge Hotel: from 10am daily

Refreshments
The Story Bridge Hotel is a good place to stop for lunch or a drink, but why not pick up some supplies from Tognini's delicatessen and bistro next door and have a picnic in Captain John Burke Park?

Route Notes
The City Council has removed some of the unstable rock and opened up parts of the cliffs for climbing, so energetic people may like to do a spot of abseiling. For those who don't know the difference, abseilers go from the top to the bottom while rock climbers do it contrariwise, but the climb can be done in any direction with the help of the Outdoors Pursuits Group (3397 7779 for information). The difficulty of the climbs ranges from 9 to 26, on an absolute scale of 1 – 32. Regular climbers range from eight-year-olds (who have to be big enough for the safety harness to do up) to active septuagenarians.

There are public toilets in Captain John Burke Park under the Story Bridge, and at the Captain Cook Bridge end of the river bank walk.

function centre, with the redoubtable Bernadette O'Shea regularly conducting her French champagne appreciation courses here. With its odd array of added wings and stand-alone buildings it is something of a shambles today, but parts of it are in the process of restoration, and a wander through the grounds to see the front of the building that faces the river is well worth an extra ten minutes.

The views of the river with the CityCats regularly making their way up and down are particularly fine. Past Yungaba, and extending across the point, is **Captain John Burke Park |7|**, a popular spot for picnics and weddings. It is named after the first resident of the area, the controller of a coastal shipping company who built a house here in the late 19th century.

Here you are directly beneath the Story Bridge, with uninterrupted views of **All Hallows School |8|** and the towering waterfront development across the river. Before Captain Burke built his house on this site, it was the home of a boiling-down works in the 1840s.

Along the river

Turn left and follow the town reach of the river upstream, passing the Holman Street ferry terminal and the Brisbane Jazz Club at No. 1 Annie Street, where there are gigs most Saturday and Sunday nights. Continue through the **James Warner Park |9|**, with unsurpassed views of the city. The path leads to the boardwalk at the base of the cliffs, where the fledgling colony's first

The Story Bridge Hotel

quarrying operations took place. In the quarried rocks you can see mooring rings for barges and other features associated with the early shipping trade.

Walk along the lower cliff path to the Thornton Street ferry terminal where, if you wish to end the walk, you can catch a ferry back to Edward Street or Eagle Street in the city. But for those who want to continue, it is a very easy walk along the path, beneath the historic **St Mary's Anglican Church |10|** with its sprawling rectory. In the 1870s, the early colonial governors were rowed across the river to attend church here and it is still one of the city's prettiest ecclesiastical buildings, with solid porphyry walls and a most attractive ceiling in the sanctuary, featuring angel musicians. The only access, however, is from Main Street (see Walk 8).

The prettiest part of the walk comes next. Observation decks and shelters offer striking views of the City Botanic Gardens with the buildings of the CBD towering behind them. This whole area is now a recreational park, with a collection of whimsical sculptures, many created out of early harbour and river artefacts, and natural reserves of mangrove swamps in their muddy-black blancmange. Here all kinds of activities take place, from rollerblading and cycling to just looking at the river traffic coming under the clean lines of the Captain Cook Bridge.

Continue along the river bank under the bridge until you come to the **River Plaza cross-river ferry** |11|, which goes to Edward Street, or to Gardens Point and North Quay via two stops at South Bank. The walk ends here, but it may be combined with the South Bank Parklands Walk No. 4.

Brisbane Corso, Highgate Hill & West End

A multicultural lifestyle

Start

Long walk: City Bus 7, 7a from Elizabeth Street to Brisbane Corso.
Shorter walk: City Bus 190, 198 from the corner of Adelaide and George Streets to stop 11, corner of Gladstone Road and Dornoch Terrace.

Finish

West End Markets, Melbourne Street. City Bus 190, 191, 198.

Length/Time

4 km/1.5 hours
8 km/2.5–3 hours

Access

There are some very steep stretches.

Two walks are suggested, the longer one taking in the south bank of the river at Yeronga and the Dutton Park cemetery, and the shorter walk starting at Highgate Hill. Both walks then continue through the high ridges of Highgate Hill, past old Queensland houses with magnificent views of the city, and through the fascinating residential and shopping areas of West End, the most culturally eclectic suburb in Brisbane.

Walk key

1. Brisbane Corso | **2.** Parkland | **3.** Downs Oval | **4.** The University of Queensland | **5.** Dutton Park cemetery | **6.** T. J. Doyle Park | **7.** Dornoch Terrace | **8.** Rotunda | **9.** No. 50 Dauphin Terrace | **10.** Road bridge | **11.** St Francis of Assisi Roman Catholic Church | **12.** Ethnically diverse eating houses | **13.** Boundary Street | **14.** West End Markets

The longer walk starts at the **Brisbane Corso** |1|, which runs some distance along the south bank of the Brisbane River. Walk downstream (towards the city, with the river on the left), past houses which all date from the period after the Second World War. They come in a wide variety of styles, and it is amusing to identify all the architectural influences along the way – No. 383 on the left is Swiss Chalet, followed by Spanish (377), Georgian (369), and low-set modern international (357), while on the right No. 344 is Federation, No. 340 shows a modern use of corrugated iron, and No. 324 is a modified Queenslander.

Past the houses, the Corso runs on the left along a **strip of parkland** |2| with picnic tables and toilets, and there are good views of the heavy growth of trees and the mangrove flats on the opposite bank across the river.

About one kilometre along, just past **Downs Oval** |3| on the right, some of the buildings of **The University of Queensland** |4| may be glimpsed.

An historic cemetery

Over thousands of years the Brisbane River has carved its way through cliffs and created huge bends as it wends its way down to Moreton Bay, and the **Dutton Park cemetery** |5| just ahead is situated on one of these. This is an ideal place from which to look back and get a real appreciation of the width and sweep of the river, and to see the grounds of The University of Queensland. There is a pretty little park on the river side of the cemetery, with picnic tables and a play area for children.

Walk up to Gladstone Road, either through the cemetery if your interests lie in the historical dead, of whom there are many here, or following the winding Memorial Park Drive through the **T. J. Doyle Park** |6| with its Harmony Garden at the top.

Turn left along Gladstone Road. There is not much to see, but it is good leg exercise, and half a kilometre on the right a coffee shop offers a useful place to gather your strength for the uphill stretch to Dornoch Terrace.

Dominating this end of Dornoch Terrace is Torbreck, a block of units which was Brisbane's first truly high-rise apartment block. It was built in 1960 using techniques that until then had been applied only to commercial buildings, and its great attraction at the time was its proximity to the city and its height – one effective selling technique was to take prospective buyers up in a helicopter so they could see what view they would get from the apartment they were thinking of buying. Torbreck is still the only high-rise building in this part of Brisbane, and it remains a striking, if not beautiful, landmark.

Dornoch Terrace

The shorter walk begins at the junction of Gladstone Road and **Dornoch Terrace** |7|. Dornoch Terrace, once a fashionable residential street, runs along a high ridge in a westerly direction. Its position attracted early free settlers who appreciated the views and the cool breezes, and many of their houses remain, contrasting starkly with the less attractive later houses and the 'six-pack' blocks of brick units that were a feature of the soulless 1950s and 1960s.

On the left is Highview (No. 189), a 1930s unit block with barley sugar columns and leadlight windows in a strange diagonal pattern; and on the right, in a small park with an **enchanting rotunda |8|**, there are fine views of the city to the east and to the Taylor Ranges, dominated by Mount Coot-tha and its television towers, to the west.

There was nothing predictable about the architecture of the 1930s, and on the left Rudmaun is distinguished by its long scalloped stucco façade, while next-but-one an eccentric conical tiled roof sits on top of an arched entrance, the red brick arch inset with blocks of tuff.

Turn left into Dauphin Terrace, where there are handsome old timber houses, well maintained, on each corner of Monto Street. Dauphin Terrace divides beyond Monto Street, so take the lower branch on the left and follow it to a blind end where **No. 50 |9|**, a 1996 copy of an early colonial house, manages to look quite convincing in its landscaped garden high above the river.

On the way to No. 50, a deep rainforest gully backs onto the houses on the left and runs down to the river, suggesting how the terrain must have appeared to the early settlers, and remaining as a rare and valuable pocket of untouched jungle close to the city centre. Return to Dornoch Terrace for more fascinating old houses.

Route Notes

Toilets in T. J. Doyle Park. The terrain is steep — these places are not called Highgate Hill and Hill End for nothing, so the walk is best undertaken on a cool day.

Refreshments

There is a coffee shop in Gladstone Road just past T. J. Doyle Park, and a plethora of eating and drinking establishments in West End, at the end of the walk.

On the right, No. 132 has a semicircular fretwork timber panel above the front door, and three chimneypots, always an indication of the importance of a Brisbane house. On the left, the low-set No. 127 has particularly fine timber steps; No. 121, built in 1920 for a Lutheran pastor who had just retired from New Guinea, has now been restored to what must surely be more than its original glory; and No. 117 is classic federation style with a red-tiled roof.

High-set views

Soon Dornoch Terrace crosses Boundary Street, which runs through a deep cutting underneath. From **the road bridge |10|** there is a wonderful view of the city on one side, and of the St Lucia reach of the river and The University of Queensland campus on the other. From here Dornoch Terrace starts to slope downwards past more houses of architectural interest – note especially Nos. 78, 74 and 68, where a later stucco facing has concealed the original verandahs and front entrance.

Lower down still on the left is the red brick bulk of the **St Francis of Assisi Roman Catholic Church |11|** and No. 37, a fine old Federation house close to a particularly unfortunate block of high-rise units. The pretty cottage at No. 33 has been effectively restored in newly fashionable heritage colours of ochre and deep burgundy.

Where Dornoch Terrace soon turns right into Hardgrave Road, a short stretch of **ethnically diverse eating houses |12|** gives way to residential dwellings less affluent

West End Markets

than those in Dornoch Terrace, an eclectic blend of the old and the new, the gentrified and the doggedly ordinary.

Towards the end of Hardgrave Road there are more places to eat, including Brisbane's cheapest and best Vietnamese restaurant, Kim Thanh. At the Vulture Street intersection, on the left corner, is another institution, Mick's Nuts, which has the freshest macadamias in town.

Eclectic shopping

Turn right into Vulture Street, passing Cambridge Street on the right, and going through the main shopping centre of West End, where the shops echo the cultural diversity of the residents. Most of these are worth exploring, if only to smell the wonderful mix of aromas emanating from the Halal delicatessen, the Vietnamese hot bread shop, the coffee merchant, the Greek delicatessen and the Asian supermarket.

At the intersection with **Boundary Street** |13| turn left, where the shops become more sophisticated, but just as culturally exciting – there's a very fine bookshop, The Avid Reader, right next to Espressohead, which coffee afficionados swear by. Their avocado on sourdough toast is always worth stopping for, too.

At the end of Boundary Street, cross the roundabout to the **West End Markets** |14|, handsomely converted in the early 1980s from an old lemonade factory. Its fortunes have been mixed, and the small shops come and go, but its customers give a genuine indication of the suburb's demographic make-up.

Go back to the roundabout and walk along Melbourne Street towards the city. There is a bus stop 250 metres along to take you back into the city, but it is only one extra kilometre to walk past the Queensland Cultural Centre and South Bank and over the Victoria Bridge into the Queen Street Mall.

Walk key

1. Red Cross Blood Bank |
2. Story Bridge |
3. Marriott Hotel |
4. Jameson's Bar and Bistro | 5. Water Police Headquarters |
6. Kangaroo Point |
7. Customs House |
8. Pier 2 | 9. Riverside Centre | 10. Riverside Markets | 11. Inlet |
12. Eagle Street Pier |
13. Yacht marina |
14. Queen's Park gates

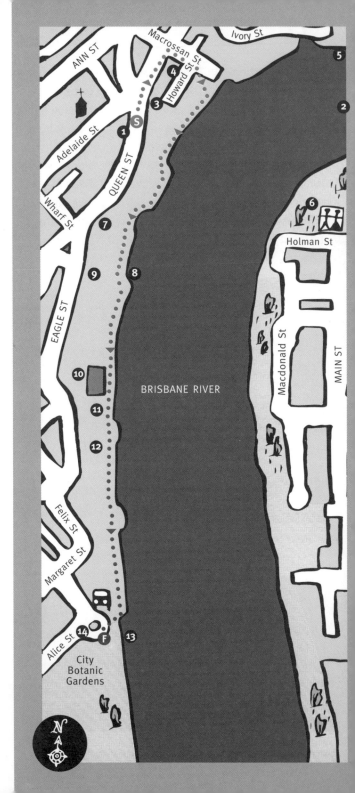

CBD River Front

Up the lazy river

Start

Queen Street, opposite the Marriott Hotel. Catch any bus along Elizabeth Street, and get off at the stop marked Circular Quay, near the Blood Bank.

Finish

City Botanical Gardens, Queens Park gates, from where there are regular buses back into the city centre.

Length/Time

1.5 km/0.5 hour

Tips

In summer, it is best to do this walk in the afternoon, when the whole area is in shade. In winter, mornings are better.

Access

The Boardwalk is gently graded and very easy going. This walk is suitable for wheelchairs.

For over a hundred years, the Brisbane River divided the city. With few bridges to link the north and south sides, there were almost two separate communities. Ten years ago, however, a far-sighted Lord Mayor, by using the term River City, struck a chord in the increasingly cosmopolitan population, and since then both sides of the city have turned their faces to the river instead of away from it. This walk goes along the boardwalk of the busiest and most effective river front development, with great restaurants, outstanding views and a happy mixture of the old and the new, of natural and built landscapes.

The walk starts in Queen Street. As you get off the bus at the **Red Cross Blood Bank |1|**, look left for an uninterrupted view of Brisbane's major landmark, the steel cantilevered **Story Bridge |2|**, designed by J. C. Bradfield, the engineer responsible for the Sydney Harbour Bridge. The towers on each side of the river were built first, while the decking extended from both sides simultaneously and, as Bill Scott notes in his entertaining book *Portrait of Brisbane*, a man was employed to row his skiff constantly under the bridge during construction, in case any of the workmen fell into the river.

Opened in 1940, it was originally called the Jubilee Bridge to commemorate King George V's Silver Jubilee, but even in those early days there was an unvoiced republican consciousness in Queensland, so that civil servants eventually took precedence over British royalty. Today the bridge is framed by blocks of luxury high-rise units, built to accommodate the increasing numbers of business people wanting to enjoy inner-city living.

Modern living

Cross the road and walk past the **Marriott Hotel |3|**, with its fountain by local sculptor Rhyl Hinwood showing figures of a young Murri couple. Continue down Adelaide Street, past old warehouses dating from the late 19th century, and the very trendy **Jameson's Bar and Bistro |4|**, quiet during the day, but swinging with the well-heeled young and restless at night.

This is increasingly the home of upmarket cafes and restaurants, and for future reference you should take note of E'cco, further up on the left on the corner of Boundary Street, which consistently wins awards for being one of the best bistros in Australia. Don't walk up as far as this, however, but turn right into Macrossan Street, and walk between the high-rise blocks of Admiralty Quays on the left and Admiralty Towers on the right, to reach the boardwalk along the river.

From here, if you look left, the Story Bridge is visible again. The tiled roof of the **Water Police Headquarters |5|** nestles below it, and the olive-green Government Stores sprawl along at the bottom of the cliffs. On the other side of the river is **Kangaroo Point |6|**, with its fresh green park (named after the earliest resident on the site, Captain John Burke, who controlled a major shipping company in the late 19th century) meandering down to one of the few popular beaches left along the river bank.

Turn right and go along the boardwalk towards the Eagle Street Pier, passing Admiralty Towers and Walter's Wine Bar. One of the few colonial buildings still standing along the river front is the old **Customs House |7|** with its impressive copper dome, built in Victorian free classical style. Begun in 1886 and finished in 1889, it is now owned by The University of Queensland, and contains a small art gallery, bookshop and a riverfront café. Below the Customs House are the remains of the original wooden pier, and a wall made of porphyry stone. The windows lead into the rooms once occupied by the customs searchers in the 1890s.

A little further along the boardwalk is the ferry stop at **Pier 2 |8|**. Here the No. 6 cross-river ferry goes to Holman Street at Kangaroo Point, and one variation of this walk is to catch this ferry and continue with the Kangaroo Point Walk No. 16.

The Riverside Centre

Walk No. 18 continues along to the **Riverside Centre |9|**, designed by Harry Seidler and perhaps the most impressive of the tall office and residential blocks that line the river. A massive flight of steps sweeps down to the river on either side of a stepped fountain, a favourite meeting place for the passing parade of people who flock here every weekend for the busy **Riverside Markets |10|**.

Michael Platsis's long-established restaurant Michael's is in this complex, with unsurpassed views of the river and the Story Bridge, but it is just as beautiful (and a lot cheaper) to sit at the bottom of the steps and feast your eyes on the river with its flotilla of cheeky ferry boats, paddle-wheelers, cargo boats and the stately City-Cats. Look up river towards the bridge and you will see the 19th century turrets of All Hallows School, now overshadowed by the apricot heights of Admiralty Wharf. Just before the Eagle Street Pier is a pretty little **inlet |11|**, with another of the sandy beaches that were once common along the

Opening Times

Cafés and restaurants along the Boardwalk are open from mid-morning until late every day. The City Botanical Gardens are open 24 hours a day.

Refreshments

The boardwalk is studded with cafés, wine bars and eating houses to suit all tastes and budgets.

Route Notes

For a longer walk, combine this with the City Botanic Gardens Walk No. 2, which will take another two hours.

river bends. The constant dredging necessary to keep the river navigable by modern boats has (unfortunately) meant that most of these beaches have now disappeared.

Here the boardwalk becomes a bridge, and passes by the remains of an old brick tunnel and slipways, some of the few reminders that this stretch of the river was once a busy customs port.

It is worth taking a break at **Eagle Street Pier |12|**, a bustling area of coffee shops, elegant restaurants and boutiques, where the two modern paddlewheelers, the *River Queen I* and *II*, are moored. Both boats offer morning or afternoon tea cruises, but the best time to go is at night on the dinner cruise, where you can lean over the side and watch the water splashing off the great paddle wheel at the back, and forget that it is there purely for decoration, the boats being motor-driven.

Across the river are the Kangaroo Point cliffs, in the early days of white settlement the site of the fledgling shipbuilding industry, which used timber from downstream. These days the bottom of the cliffs is a picnic area, and if you look carefully you can usually see tiny figures abseiling down from the top or climbing up from the bottom.

Of the many good restaurants on this stretch of the river, the eponymous Pier Nine consistently wins awards for the best seafood restaurant of the year, so if it is lunchtime and you are feeling flush, try a plate of their mixed oysters and check out the very superior lavatories.

Town Reach Brisbane River

Across the river

From here, it is possible to see a few original houses among the proliferating units across the river at Kangaroo Point, as well as the little stone Anglican church of St Mary's, Kangaroo Point, and the casual sprawl of the rectory with its wide verandahs. A look back at All Hallows School presents an entirely different ecclesiastical picture, however, as from this angle the building looks more like a medieval fortress than a young ladies' college.

A little further along are the calm moorings of the **yacht marina |13|**, where up to 54 sleek creatures sun themselves in the morning light on one of the best protected reaches of the river, only a dinghy ride away from the city – it is enough to make the most dedicated landlubber salivate. And all for $15 a week! These are casual moorings only, and they house a shifting cosmopolitan community, with sailors from all over the world taking refuge here for a few weeks before moving on.

Officials of the Port of Brisbane Corporation are adamant that yachties are the cleanest people on the water, with immaculate onshore facilities made available to them by Heritage Holdings.

This area, which a century ago was occupied by timber wharves where passengers and cargoes were unloaded, is best seen from the lower path of the boardwalk, but the high path takes you past the temptations of the Heritage Hotel and its riverfront brasserie.

Both paths converge at the beginning of the City Botanic Gardens – go up the ferry ramp and turn left for the **Queen's Park gates** |14| at the Edward Street entrance. From here, either continue with the City Botanic Gardens Walk No. 2 or return to the city. Bus 23 leaves this point every 15 minutes from Monday to Friday, but does not operate at weekends. It is an easy four-block walk to Elizabeth Street in the city centre.

Toowong to the City along the River

Boats and bridges

Start

Regatta Hotel, Coronation Drive – Rocket Bus 407, or City Bus 412 from the corner of Adelaide and George Streets.

Finish

Victoria Bridge or, for a longer walk, add Walk 2.

Length/Time

4 km/1.5 hours
(to Victoria Bridge)

Access & Tips

No steps, and the few slopes are suitable for wheelchairs. Take a bottle of water and a hat.

At 5.30am, with the sun struggling through the clouds, the power walkers are out on the Toowong bikeway. By 8am the cyclists have taken over. Mid-morning is parents-and-strollers' time, while late in the afternoon people walk their dogs, little kids learn to balance on their new rollerblades, and courting couples of all ages stroll arm in arm. From dawn to dusk, the river bank is humming with life, and it can be seen at its most beautiful on this easy walk from the suburb of Toowong into the centre of the city.

Walk key

1. Regatta Hotel | 2. Path along the river bank | 3. Tall pines | 4. Wesley Hospital | 5. Gas stripping tower | 6. Oxley's on the River | 7. Cook Terraces | 8. William Jolly Bridge | 9. Kurilpa Point Park | 10. Brisbane Transit Centre | 11. The Cairn | 12. Victoria Bridge | 13. Queensland Cultural Centre | 14. Performing Arts Complex | 15. South Bank Parklands | 16. Convention Centre | 17. Commissariat Stores | 18. Parliament House | 19. Queensland University of Technology

Begin your walk at the heritage-listed **Regatta Hotel** |1|, a long-time favourite watering hole for university students and staff of the Australian Broadcasting Corporation situated just up the road on the river bank.

The Regatta was built in 1886, and still retains its iron-lace verandahs and colonial splendour, the latter somewhat dimmed because of its position on busy Coronation Drive, which, after the great flood of 1974, was diverted to ease traffic pressure on the main road into the city. During the flood the Brisbane River broke its banks and the Regatta was flooded up to the first-floor balcony. The ferry terminal that once stood here, to serve passengers and ABC employees crossing the river to the ABC's other recording studios in Ferry Road, West End, was washed away in the floods and never re-instated, to the disappointment of many residents.

Across the road from the Regatta Hotel, walk down to the **path along the river bank** |2|. The earlier you take your walk, the better chance you have of seeing boats from the GPS Rowing Club and the South Brisbane Sailing Club at practice, sometimes with their panting coaches running up and down the path yelling heated instructions through a megaphone.

The **tall pines** |3| on the southern bank of the river opposite the Regatta Hotel were noted by John Oxley, the first white explorer to sail up the river.

The next landmark on the north bank is the **Wesley Hospital** |4|, a private hospital built on land once owned by the Mayne family, who were the great benefactors of the nearby University of Queensland. Their family home, Moorlands, was built in 1892 as a private house for Mrs Mary Mayne, widow of a Queen Street butcher who made his fortune in an age before the Heart Foundation put red meat on the forbidden list. There has always been a mystery about the Mayne family, which Rosamund Siemon finally solved in her fascinating book *The Mayne Inheritance*. Moorlands is now used as the administration offices of Wesley Hospital, and has been listed by the National Trust.

Look across the river to the **gas stripping tower** |5| on the south bank, which was used to remove tar and ammonia from coal gas. It was brought out from Yorkshire in 1912 and restored by the National Trust in 1980. Next to the gas tower is the boat shed belonging to Brisbane Grammar School.

Oxley's on the River |6| is a true floating restaurant, built on piles so it rises and falls with the tides (the Brisbane River is tidal as far as Mt Crosby, many kilometres upstream). The Pit Stop, its little coffee shop, is a good place to stop for a cold drink, or even lunch if you're walking in the heat of the day. (See Refreshments.)

Cook Terraces |7| on the north bank, now housing business services as well as a glass-walled restaurant and bar, are some of the city's few remaining terraces, and were built in 1888.

In the spring and summer there are flowering jacarandas, poincianas, coral trees and tulip trees, and of course plenty of frangipani and hibiscus. All these are introduced varieties, adding splashes of brilliance to the various greens of the indigenous palms, hoop and Bunya pines, blue gums, weeping figs and Moreton Bay figs along the river bank.

The bridges

As you approach the city the bridges begin. Only ten bridges have been built across the 336 kilometre length of the Brisbane River, and five of them are in the CBD. The modern Merivale Railway Bridge won an engineering design award in 1978, but next to it the **William Jolly Bridge |8|** (known to locals as the Grey Street Bridge and opened to traffic in 1932), with its rainbow arches and concrete casings surfaced to look like porphyry stone, beats it hands down for sheer beauty.

Look across the river now to the south bank to see an outstanding example of imaginative river bank rejuvenation. **Kurilpa Point Park |9|**, named after the water rat, was once an eyesore, a run-down industrial area, but as part of the City Council's policy of beautification of the river front, in the last three years it has been cleaned up and transformed into a very pretty place, with picnic tables and attractive gardens.

Now you are approaching the city proper. Behind the Police Headquarters can be seen the black glass tower of the **Brisbane Transit Centre |10|**, where interstate trains and buses terminate. Many people consider it as much of an eyesore as Kurilpa

Opening Times

Commissariat Stores, 115 William Street: Tues, Wed, Thur 10am–4pm, Fri 11am–2pm.
Parliament House: open for tours only when Parliament is not sitting (3406 7562 for details).

Refreshments

The only place on the cycle path itself is the Pit Stop Café at Oxley's on the River, open from 10.30am.

Route Notes

This path is designed for cyclists as well as pedestrians, who should take care not to get in the way of over-enthusiastic university students running late for lectures.

Point used to be, but it has at least centralised public transport in an increasingly congested city.

The buildings that flank the river for the next few blocks are mainly offices, hotels and law courts. The path slopes downwards at this point under the sweep of the Riverside Expressway, and if you want to see **the cairn |11|** marking the place where explorer John Oxley stopped for water and decided that this would be an ideal place for a settlement, you have to leave the path and walk up to the corner of North Quay and Makerston Street.

The Victoria Bridge

Under the expressway, the muddy remains of the mangrove swamps that once lined the banks of the river seem years away from the traffic thundering overhead, but the path soon comes into the open air as it approaches the **Victoria Bridge |12|** at Queen Street, built where the very first bridge across the river was constructed in 1865. That wooden structure lasted for two years, before succumbing to the tender attentions of marine borers and collapsing just after the Cobb & Co. coach from Ipswich had passed over it. The second bridge was opened in 1874, but was severely damaged by the great floods of 1893 and 1896, and a 'new' Victoria Bridge was opened in 1896.

Today's bridge was completed in 1969, and here you will find an active little shipping centre, with ferry terminals for the CityCat, cross-river ferries, and private

Victoria Bridge

charter boats and barges. This is where the *Mirimar*, which goes up-river to the Lone Pine Koala Sanctuary, is moored. Across the river are the strange and varied buildings that make up the **Queensland Cultural Centre |13|** – just before the Victoria Bridge are the monumental grey bunkers of the State Library, the Queensland Art Gallery with the Queensland Museum just behind it, and the beautiful lawns of the QEII Park. Another boardwalk and cycle path follow the river bank on this side.

On the other side of the bridge is the **Performing Arts Complex |14|**, part of the original design by architect Robin Gibson, which houses the Lyric Theatre, Concert Hall, the very new Playhouse Theatre and a smaller studio theatre called the Cremorne. This complex extends into the **South Bank Parklands** |15|, where the Conservatorium of Music, the oddly shaped *IMAX* theatre and the curves of the **Convention Centre** |16| make up a strangely assorted conglomeration of buildings which do not always seem to sit happily together.

Just past the Victoria Bridge on the north side are the **Commissariat Stores** |17|, built by convict labour in 1929 during the regime of the notorious Captain Logan, with a third storey added in 1913. Along with the Tower Mill (see Walk No. 3), this is the oldest building in Brisbane. It is open to the public (see Opening Times).

It is just possible to see from the river path the beautiful old **Parliament House** |18| of 1868 (also open to the public – see Opening Times), overlooked but never overshadowed by the excrescence of the new building, a legacy of the 1970s when progress rather than beauty or heritage was the buzzword.

The walk ends at the **Queensland University of Technology** |19| and the City Botanic Gardens, the breathing green heart of the city, which have been Brisbane's quiet retreat since 1865.

The CityCat stops here, to take you up or downriver or back into the CBD, and there is a cross-river ferry to South Bank Parklands. You can continue with the City Botanic Gardens Walk No. 2 in reverse order, or else it is a leisurely fifteen-minute stroll back into the centre of the city.

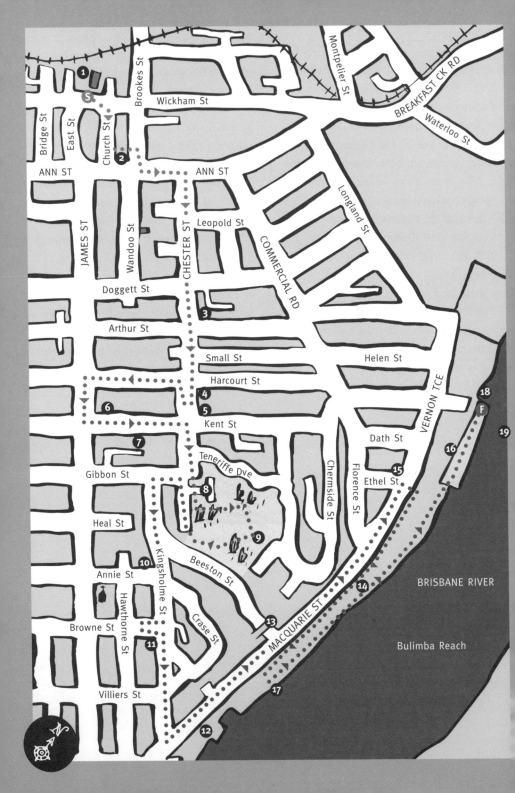

Teneriffe & the Old Wharves

New life for old

Start

Wickham Street, Fortitude Valley. City Bus 470 from North Quay or Elizabeth Street, or City Bus 300 from the corner of Adelaide and Edward Streets. Get off at stop 6 near the Valley Baths.

Finish

Corner of Vernon Terrace and Commercial Road. Return to the city either by ferry or City Bus 470 from the ferry terminal.

Length/Time

4.5 km/1.5 hours

Access

The area is hilly and difficult for wheelchairs.

The wharves at Teneriffe are some of the oldest on the river. In the late 19th century Brisbane was a bustling maritime centre, but eventually the wharves and warehouses were abandoned. Now, however, as part of the City Council's Urban Renewal program, the old warehouses are coming to life again as smart new apartment blocks, and many of the pretty workers' cottages in the adjoining suburbs are being restored and gentrified. This walk gives a good indication of the subtropical domestic architecture of the early 20th century, as well as a sense of Brisbane's maritime history.

Walk key

1. Valley Baths | 2. Holy Trinity Church precinct | 3. Unrestored shop building | 4. Town house | 5. Roseville | 6. Old shop with its original verandahs | 7. No. 215 Kent Street | 8. Little Chester Street | 9. Teneriffe Park | 10. Old Queenslander | 11. Browne Street | 12. Riverside Coal Transport buildings | 13. Wool Stores | 14. Teneriffe Wharves | 15. Australian Mercantile Land and Finance Company | 16. Sir Manuel Hornibrook Park | 17. Old wharves | 18. Teneriffe ferry terminal | 19. Bulimba terminal

Get off the bus at the **Valley Baths** |1| and cross Wickham Street at Church Street, going through the **Holy Trinity church precinct** |2| (see Walk No. 5 for details) to Brookes Street, and turning left into Ann Street. The first main street on the right is Chester Street where, after some dull commercial buildings, comes an interesting mix of domestic dwellings.

On the left, on the corner of Arthur Street, an **unrestored shop building** |3| with a roofed verandah sheltering the footpath offers a reminder of days when town planners were more aware of the needs of pedestrians. Diagonally opposite the shop is an old Queenslander, restored more successfully than the mock colonial house on the corner of Harcourt Street, with its unnecessarily ornate fence. A **town house** |4| on the opposite corner of Harcourt Street provides a striking modern contrast, with its orange, yellow and purple exterior walls.

Before turning right into Harcourt Street, walk halfway along the next block of Chester Street to see **Roseville** |5| (1885), one of the most elegant old homes in the area, which has for years been a restaurant and reception centre.

Harcourt Street

The trees which line both sides of Harcourt Street add an extra touch of softness to the mix of workers' cottages, many of which have been gentrified, more or less successfully. As in other Australian capital cities, many of the inner-city working class suburbs have now been taken over by young profes-sionals, which makes them smarter and probably safer, but to a large extent has taken away their original rough charm.

Nos. 266 and 260 are worth a close look, and on the other side of the road the restored house at No. 251 makes an interesting contrast to its practically untouched neighbour at No. 249. No. 256 is an example of the insensitive modernisation that took place during the 1960s, but the modern townhouse at 258 shows how old and new can blend harmoniously in this street of architectural contrasts.

From Harcourt, turn left into James Street (not much to see here) and left again into Kent, where another **old shop with its original verandahs** |6| is still operating as a convenience store – a good place to stock up on bottled water, as the next part of the walk contains a number of hills.

In Kent Street, notice the bull-nosed verandah roof and the wide chamfer boards at **No. 215** |7|, which indicate that the house is quite early, probably around the turn of the 19th century. The iron roof on No. 233 may well be original, and it sports a rare brick chimney, indicating that this was once a house of some importance. Next door, No. 237 has timber balustrades with some unusual geometric patterning, while the modern house at No. 241, with its ochre walls and pink fence, shows how a very large house can be made to sit comfortably on a block with a narrow street frontage.

Turn right into Chester Street, and continue up a rather steep hill to Little Chester Street, noticing two lovely old houses at No. 79 and 81, the latter best seen from the bottom of the hill, as its delicate iron-lace ridge cap and finials are hidden by the high front fence. Across the road, the very high-set house at No. 80 is an example of how Brisbane people value the breeze as well as the views.

A well-kept secret

Little Chester Street |8| is one of Brisbane's hidden secrets. The dead-end street, with its row of cottages on the ridge overlooking the river and the old Goldsborough Mort Wool Stores, runs alongside the grassy knoll of **Teneriffe Park |9|**. Here, the gnarled roots of ancient fig trees support the high bank, mangoes and jacarandas mix happily with the indigenous hoop pines, the children's play area is sheltered under a huge sun sail, and even the picnic gazebo has its own special 1930s charm.

Return to Chester Street and take an immediate left turn into Gibbon Street and another into Beeston. From here it is downhill, but where Beeston Street swings to the left, take the right fork into Kingsholme Street. At the corner of Crase Street, look back (or make a slight detour) to see a really lovely **old Queenslander |10|** on the corner of Annie Street, and further down Kingsholme notice a genuine two-storey house on the corner of Villiers Street. This is a rare find in this area, as most double-storey houses are basically stilt buildings where the underneath was built in much later.

Follow Kingsholme Street down to the river, noticing along the way some of the

Refreshments

Aqua Linea is one of the many elegant modern bars right on the river in the newly developed **Teneriffe Wharves** complex. There is a convenience store in Kent Street.

more elaborate houses, too big to be called cottages. Past Crase Street, Kingsholme divides into an upper and a lower carriageway, with the houses on the high side built on stilts to get an even better view of the river and the city. In **Browne Street |11|** on the right is a house so out of character with the rest of the buildings that it seems to be an escapee from one of the southern capitals like Melbourne or Sydney.

From Kingsholme Street, turn left at the bottom of the hill into Macquarie Street, which used to be lined with warehouses and wharves. The monumental red or cream brick warehouses are still there, but many have taken on a new lease of life as trendy apartments, a demographic transformation which, further along the street, has brought a rash of coffee shops and bars in its wake.

Wharves and warehouses

The still-active **Riverside Coal Transport buildings |12|**, across Macquarie Street on the right, prove that the mercantile life of this area has not completely succumbed to gentrification.

The old **Wool Stores |13|** of 1926, where wool bales were stored before being shipped overseas, retain something of their grandeur, even though they have come down in the world in their new incarnation as a series of furniture shops. They make a pleasing contrast to the multi-unit riverfront developments at No. 135 Macquarie Street, where the old **Teneriffe Wharves |14|** have been given a new lease of life.

Fig trees in Teneriffe Park

Past the corner of Florence Street, Macquarie becomes Vernon Terrace, where a large antiques and decorative arts centre now occupies the old **Australian Mercantile Land and Finance Company |15|**. This commanding building is best seen from across the road, where its splendid proportions are more apparent, so cross over to the Teneriffe Wharves complex and the cheerful Aqua Linea Bar, where you will appreciate a cold drink while admiring the Mercantile Building.

From here, wander down to the boardwalk through **Sir Manuel Hornibrook Park |16|** and stroll along upstream, noticing the working shipyards on the other bank, as well as a mixture of old and nouveau-riche houses with their private moorings. The boardwalk goes up river for about 300 metres and then comes to a dead end, but it's worth the stroll for the breezes, the views and, if you're interested in **old wharves |17|**, a rare glimpse of 19th century pylons and tidal flats in their more Dickensian aspect.

Return along the boardwalk to the **Teneriffe ferry terminal |18|** and catch City Bus 470 back to the city. To return by boat, catch the tiny cross-river ferry here to the restored **Bulimba terminal |19|**, where you can get the CityCat back into the CBD. There is no accessible CityCat stop on this section of the north river bank.

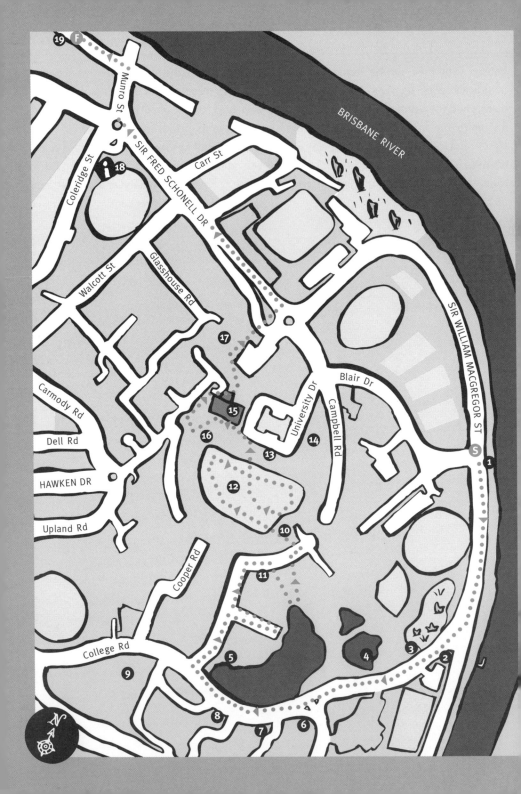

BRISBANE RIVER

SIR WILLIAM MACGREGOR ST

Munro St

Coleridge St

SIR FRED SCHONELL DR

Carr St

Walcott St

Glasshouse Rd

Carmody Rd

Dell Rd

HAWKEN DR

Upland Rd

Cooper Rd

College Rd

University Dr

Blair Dr

Campbell Rd

19 F

18 i

17

15

16

13

14

12

10

11

9

5

4

3

2

1 S

8

7

6

N

The University of Queensland, St Lucia

Academic arcadia

Start

Corner of McGregor and Blair Drives, at The University of Queensland CityCat terminal.

Finish

Guyatt Park on the river. Catch the CityCat ferry (Rocket 407) or City Bus 411, 412 or rocket bus 407 back to the city.

Length/Time

3 km/1.5 hours, plus time spent in museums and cafés.

Access & Tips

An easy walk with plenty of shade. The grounds and all the buildings are wheelchair accessible.

Queensland's first and largest university was established in 1909, but the present site was not acquired until 1926, when the Mayne family gave the university 114 hectares of farmland on a bend in the Brisbane River. The first completed building, the Forgan Smith, was diverted to military purposes during the Second World War and teaching did not begin here until 1946. This walk begins on the flood plains of the Brisbane River, continues through the well-established gardens and takes in some of the older buildings, especially the Great Court.

Walk key

1. University of Queensland CityCat stop | 2. Statue of St Vladimir | 3. Alumni Teaching Garden | 4. Small lakes | 5. Engineering Building | 6. Women's College | 7. Duchesne | 8. St Leo's | 9. St John's | 10. Wordsmiths Café | 11. Staff House | 12. Great Court | 13. Forgan Smith Building | 14. Mayne Library | 15. Mayne Hall | 16. Chancellor's Place | 17. Hartley Teakle Building | 18. Information Booth | 19. Guyatt Park

Take the CityCat to the **University of Queensland stop |1|** (after Guyatt Park and West End) and walk along Sir William McGregor Drive, with the river on your left. Across the river, there are a number of fine old houses built among the thick vegetation on the high river bank. This part of the university was badly affected by the great flood of 1974, but houses on the Hill End/West End banks were unaffected.

Parks and playing fields

On the right, across the playing fields, the Schonell Cinema, the Student Union complex, and some of the university's more modern buildings can be seen. About 500 metres along, turn right into College Road, where a **statue of St Vladimir |2|**, donated by the Russian community of Brisbane to mark the bicentenary of white settlement in Australia, was unveiled by the Governor General, Bill Hayden, in 1995. On the right is the **Alumni Teaching Garden |3|**. This area of lush rainforest, with its walkways and tiny creeks, gives an idea of what the original vegetation of this area may have been like, and curious lizards, birds and even small mammals can often be seen if visitors walk quietly and keep their voices down.

Continue along College Road and past **two small lakes |4|** on your right, which are surrounded by the Una Prentice Memorial Gardens, honouring the university's first woman law graduate. If you take this walk in October, you will experience one of the great delights of Brisbane in the spring, an avenue of ancient jacaranda trees in their full purple glory.

It is tempting to wander along the paths by these lakes and feed the ducks and other wild fowl, but be wary of the ganders which have also taken up residence there – they can be very aggressive, especially if you have food in your hands.

Just past the two small lakes is a much larger lake which contains a fountain and the skeletons of trees drowned when the lake was established. Late in the afternoon flocks of white ibis come to roost in these trees, forming a mass of living white foliage. On the far side of this lake a new section of the **Engineering Building |5|** gives an indication of the university's never-ending building program.

On the left side of College Road you will see most of the university's student residential colleges – in order, **Women's |6|** (non-denominational female), **Duchesne |7|** (Roman Catholic female) and **St Leo's |8|** (Roman Catholic male).

Rather than going past the next college, **St John's |9|** (Anglican, female and male), turn right into Staff House Road. Turn right again into Jock's Road for a different view of the lake, and perhaps take a detour down to its edge, where a wooden bench commemorates Dr Eunice Hanger, long-time staff member of the English Department and benefactor of the university.

Staff House Road

Retrace your steps along Jock's Road and into Staff House Road again, following it around to the right. On the left are the popular **Wordsmiths Café |10|** and the University Bookshop, and on the right is the **Staff House |11|**, home of the University of Queensland Staff and Graduates Club – members only. Just past the Staff House take a detour down the wide steps to expansive gardens also leading down to the lake. Look back to the road for an overall idea of the diversity of the university's buildings, and return to Staff House Road, stopping at Wordsmiths Café to admire the stone sculptures of Australian writers and their works by Rhyl Hinwood. The centrepiece of this sculpture collection is a bench in Helidon sandstone featuring the Rainbow Serpent of Murri legend and a quotation from the work of Queensland's most important indigenous poet, Oodgeroo of the tribe Noonuccul – 'To our children's children, the glad tomorrow'.

The Great Court

At the back of Wordsmiths Café is a set of steps leading into the **Great Court |12|**, an elegant collection of buildings faced with local Helidon sandstone. Dating from 1937, they have been heritage listed by the National Trust of Queensland.

Of particular interest are the cloisters, where coats of arms of other universities, grotesques of distinguished members of the university, and native fauna decorate the walls and pillars. From 1939 to 1953 these were sculpted by John Theodore Muller, and his work is now being continued by Rhyl Hinwood.

Opening Times

The grounds are accessible 24 hours a day, and most faculty buildings are open from early morning to early evening. Shops and cafés on campus have flexible hours depending on the academic year. Ring the university switchboard on 3365 1111 for more details.

Zoology Museum: Mon–Fri 9am–4pm (3365 8548)

Physics Museum: Tue 1pm–2pm during semester (3365 3424)

Anthropology Museum: Tue–Thur 11am–3pm during semester (3365 1214)

Antiquities Museum: Mon–Fri 9am–1pm, 2pm–5pm (3365 2643)

University Art Museum: Mon–Fri 10am–5pm (3365 3046)

Geology Museum: Mon–Fri 9am–4pm (3365 2668)

Route Notes

Although there are regular buses to the university from the city, a more relaxing way to arrive at the campus is on the CityCat ferry, which provides a very different perspective on the area. CityCat services run every 30 minutes, and in the CBD the ferries stop at North Quay, QUT Gardens Point and Riverside. For more detail about the activities of The University of Queensland, the colourful 'Guide for Visitors' brochure with map is available at the Information Booth on the Schonell Drive/Coleridge Street roundabout, or at the J. D. Story Administration building behind the Michie Building on the Great Court.

Refreshments

Student refectory services are open during semester, with the main refectory also open during vacations from 8.30am–3pm.

There is an open-air café near the bookshop, a pizza café near the Schonell Cinema is open in the evenings, and there are other cafés at various places around the campus. All of these except the Staff and Graduates Club are open to the public.

Cloisters and Great Court,
the University of Queensland

There are a number of museums open to the public in different faculty buildings, most of which ring the Great Court. Walking clockwise around the Great Court you come to the Richards Building (Earth Sciences), Parnell (Physics), Goddard (Botany and Zoology), Michie (Arts), Forgan Smith (Arts), Duhig (Humanities and Social Sciences Library) and Steele (Pharmacy).

The Goddard Building houses a zoology museum with more than ten thousand specimens of Australian wildlife, collected over 85 years (see Opening Times). The Physics Museum in the Parnell Building, illustrating the context in which physics developed as a separate discipline, is open only during semester (see Opening Times). The seven-level Michie Building has two important museums. The twenty-five thousand strong collection of artefacts from Australia, Papua New Guinea and the Pacific Islands in the Anthropology Museum on Level 2 is open during semester or by appointment (see Opening Times). On Level 7 the Antiquities Museum houses artefacts spanning thirty-five hundred years of western history (see Opening Times).

The main building in the Great Court is the university's oldest, and is named the **Forgan Smith Building** |13| after the premier of the day. Its cloisters contain the most impressive sculptures, and in the tower ('A Place of Light, Liberty and Learning' as the motto proclaims), is the University Art Museum, with more than 1700 works of art, including some of Australia's leading postwar artists (see Opening Times).

At the end of the main building is the entrance to the Humanities and Social Sciences Library and Tanja's Cloisters Café in a corner of the Great Court. Continue inside the cloisters to the Steele Building for a rare collection of minerals, rocks and fossils in the acclaimed Geology Museum (see Opening Times).

At this point, retrace your steps and walk through the Forgan Smith Building to the front lawn, where you will see the **Mayne Library** |14| on the right and the modern **Mayne Hall** |15| on the left, both named after the university's generous benefactors.

From the university to the river

Go back to the Michie Building, walking between it and the Biological Sciences Library, to the bus stop in **Chancellor's Place** |16|. From here, buses run frequently to the city, but if you prefer to return on the CityCat, it is about a one-kilometre walk to the Guyatt Park stop.

To get there, cut across the lawns past Mayne Hall and the U-shaped brick **Hartley Teakle Building** |17|, and past the parking stations onto Schonell Drive, the main road into the city. Walk along Schonell Drive on the right side (the river is on your right) and turn right into Munro Street at the roundabout where the **Information Booth** |18| is situated. From Munro Street, turn left into Macquarie Street, once a pleasant backwater of low-set houses which, after the floods of 1974, were replaced by blocks of expensive high-rise units. This street follows the curve of the river (there is a cross-river ferry at the end of Laurence Street which goes across to Hill End – see Walk No. 17) and comes out at **Guyatt Park** |19|, where established trees and a children's playground provide a popular picnic place for local residents. The white theatre building on the rising ground above the car park on the left is the university's Avalon Theatre, where drama students have their practical classes. Catch the CityCat at Guyatt Park for a ten-minute ferry ride into the centre of the city.

Walk key

1. Botanic Gardens |
2. Mt Coot-tha Quarry |
3. Mt Coot-tha Lookout |
4. Graded track |
5. Aboriginal Art Trail |
6. Yellow and white painted rocks | 7. Main Gallery |
8. Dance pit | 9. Weeping figs | 10. Stuartholme School

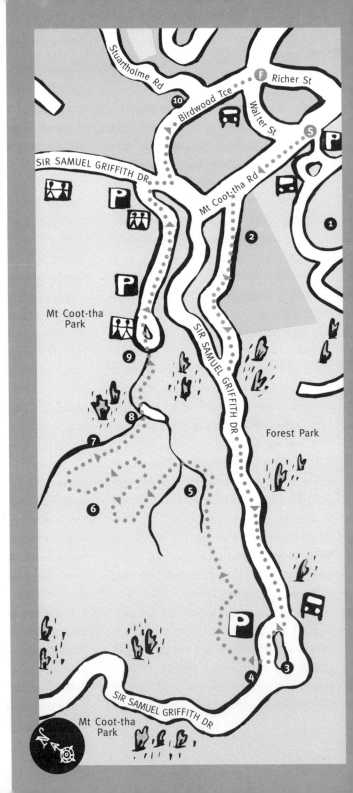

Slaughter Falls & Mt Coot-tha
The place of the honey bee

Start

Catch City Bus 471 from the corner of Adelaide and Albert Streets. Get off at the Botanic Gardens for a longer walk, or at the Mt Coot-tha Lookout for a shorter one.

Finish

At the steps of Stuartholme School in Birdwood Terrace, City Bus 410.

Length/Time

5.5 km/2.5 hours, includes 1.5 km of the Aboriginal Art Trail. 8 km/3 hours, includes the whole Aboriginal Art Trail.

Access & Tips

This is a bush walk along roads and rough trails, with many uphill sections, and not suitable for wheelchairs. Take a bottle of water, wear sensible shoes, a hat and insect repellent.

Mt Coot-tha, named after the kuta, the rich dark honey of the stingless native bee, is only five kilometres west of the CBD, and easily reached by bus. Its dramatic skyline, with the tall towers of the television transmitters, can be seen from the city. Fifteen hundred hectares of bushland have been set aside as a forest park. This walk covers some of the park and continues down to the popular picnic area along East Ithaca Creek called J. C. Slaughter Falls, named after the Brisbane Town Clerk from 1940 –1967. Much of the walk is through open eucalypt forest where nothing can be heard but bird song, running water and the wind in the trees, though the city is only a few kilometres away. The Aboriginal Art Trail, featuring contemporary artworks such as tree painting, rock painting, etchings, rock arrangements and a dance pit, is extra, but highly recommended.

For the longer walk, leave the bus at the **Botanic Gardens |1|**, turn left onto the main road and slog up the hill (this part of the walk should only be undertaken by enthusiasts or masochists), turning left at the Mt Coot-tha sign.

Below to the left is the vast **Mt Coot-tha Quarry |2|**, which is unique in being so close to the centre of a major city. Road metal has been blasted from this quarry since 1919, and there are no plans to close it down for a number of years yet. The very top of Mt Coot-tha is two kilometres further on. The road is exposed, but there are increasingly expansive views of Brisbane glimpsed through the trees.

For the short walk, make it easy on yourself by staying on the bus until it reaches the **Mt Coot-tha Lookout |3|**.

The lookout

Spend a few minutes looking at the views from the lookout platform, identifying Brisbane landmarks like The University of Queensland, the Brisbane River, the CBD, the airport and the bay islands. A large coin-operated telescope adds to the fun. This might be the time for a toilet break and to stock up on cold drinks, or to be tempted by the gift shop, which you will not be passing again.

When you are ready to start the downhill walk, continue along the road beyond the lookout for about 30 metres. Just past the last red-tiled traffic island look for a **graded track on the right |4|** going downhill, leading through pleasant eucalyptus forest to the bank of East Ithaca Creek. Watch your step on the steeper sections, as the surface can be quite loose and it is easy to slip.

Follow the track along the creek to the first crossing, where a City Council sign with useful information about the Aboriginal Art Trail directs you up to the left. For a short distance this track follows a branch of the creek, with quiet pools and huge boulders patterned with lichen. The first two works on the **Aboriginal Art Trail |5|** can be found on this part of the track. The first is a collection of ochre stencils and the second a rock painting which can be reached via wooden steps leading down to the creek bank. The path is very rough at this point, with tree roots and loose rocks, so take special care.

Further along, the path bends sharply to the right and climbs even more steeply up rock steps, where at the top is an arrangement of stones representing a serpent, one of the most important creatures in ancient Murri mythology.

At last the path begins to descend again. Look for a glimpse on the right of Stuartholme Convent, a girls' private school with a fortress-like skyline. High up in trees along the path are possum boxes, built to provide safe nesting places for these nocturnal marsupials. They are a protected species, but to many householders who find they have taken up residence inside the ceiling, or who are woken at night by their hysterical screams and thundering feet as they chase each other across the tin roof, they are nothing but a nuisance.

Aboriginal Art Trail

Ahead on the left are **rocks painted yellow and white |6|**, representing the eggs of a serpent in a riverbed. Where the path turns sharply right again, stylised kangaroo footprints have been carved into a tree trunk.

The track is now following another tributary of Ithaca Creek, and the path becomes more gradual. Stone steps on the left lead to the **Main Gallery |7|**, which features a Murri map of the area. The best way to see it in detail is to rock-hop over to it, taking care not to slip, especially in wet weather.

The creek at this point forms a series of rock pools above a low waterfall, although the only serious flows come after heavy rain. The vegetation here is dry rainforest; greener, denser and offering more shelter than the eucalyptus trees up on the higher slopes of the mountain.

Return to the Aboriginal Art Trail, which soon rejoins the main track. Turn left here and cross the creek on the large stepping stones. You may be tempted by the set of stone steps leading up the hill, but these should only be used as an alternative route if the creek is in flood.

Keep going ahead to the last Murri construction, a **dance pit |8|**, behind which is a pool where the creek has been dammed to form the Slaughter Falls.

The track has now become a road and soon crosses the creek again. Look back at this point for a good view of the Slaughter Falls which, like all falls, look their best after the heavy rains of the wet season (December to February). The road rises

Opening Times

Kuta Café at the Mt Coot-tha Lookout: 7am–11pm daily, including public holidays.

Refreshments

The Kuta Café has cold drinks, ice-creams, snacks and full meals. There are taps at the picnic areas, but carry bottled water for the dry stretches, especially during hot weather.

Route Notes

Sometimes after heavy rain during the wet season (December–January), the East Ithaca Creek may flood, although the water level does not stay high for long. If you choose to walk in these conditions, an alternative route is suggested, leading higher up the hill. Barbecues with wood supplies can be found in picnic areas at Slaughter Falls, also toilets and tap water, so why not make a day of it with a Great Australian Barbie at the end of the walk? Trail bikes and fires (except in designated barbecue areas) are prohibited in the park. All native animals and plants are protected. Keep to the walking tracks at all times to avoid disturbing the delicate ecological balance of the mountain.

gently at this point and the trees on the flat grassy area along the creek contain many inhabited possum boxes.

Reminders of the Second World War

On the right, as the road bends, is a galvanised iron igloo built into the bank, a relic of the Second World War, when the Mt Coot-tha Reserve was taken over by the US Navy and used as a munitions dump. Storerooms like this mushroomed through the bush, and although most of them were dismantled after the war, the tracks which led to them were used for entirely different purposes by many courting couples in the postwar era. These days the young find more comfortable venues, and the tracks are all but gone, closed off or taken over by the bush.

Take the steps just past the large assemblage of rocks on the left. As you cross the creek yet again, notice several large blocks of dark grey mossy concrete on the right-hand bank, the remnants of a dam wall built when the Reserve was first set aside for public use in 1880. This wall spanned the creek a few metres down from the crossing, and stood until after the Second World War, when the Brisbane City Council began to rehabilitate the area.

Once over the crossing, continue up the steps to the right. The steps on the left mark the end of the alternative wet weather route mentioned earlier. At the top of the right-hand steps is a large flat area bordered by a toilet block on the left and **a row of six tall**

Slaughter Falls

weeping figs |9|, planted in the 19th century, on the right. The shed in the middle looks just like any other picnic shelter, but the slab it stands on is another relic of the Second World War, when it formed the base of a large administration building associated with the munitions.

Walk down the stone steps on the right, just behind the fourth fig tree, and go down to the creek again. There are more concrete blocks in the creek bed, all remnants of the lower dam wall which in the 19th century retained water to form a small lake, part of an early recreational area. Long after the lower wall was destroyed in the great flood of 1893, the area was still known as The Dams. Cross the next bridge where, on the hillside on the right, a cleared platform acts as an open-air chapel, a popular place for weddings. In the middle of the car park a brass plate on a tree stump marks the Bikers Memorial, proclaiming that it was donated by the God Squad CMC.

Keep following the road downstream across four more bridges and several picnic spots, where you may see another specimen of pesky but protected wild life, brush turkeys, nonchalantly strolling by or foraging near the picnickers. These birds seem to know they are protected, for they invade suburban gardens and dig them up to make their huge nesting mounds, in defiance of the gardeners who are restricted to fruitlessly chasing them away with unprintable epithets. Cross the last bridge where there are some hundred-year-old mango trees

and one lone Bunya pine, turn right where the Slaughter Falls Road meets Sir Samuel Griffith Drive, then left again a little higher up, into Birdwood Terrace.

It is only a short walk from here to the steps of **Stuartholme School** |10| (1920). Along the way look up to the left to see the looming triangular façade of the school chapel, built in the early 1960s. During the Second World War, Stuartholme, which has always been an exclusive private school for girls, was commandeered by the US Army as a troop hospital.

The bus stop for City Bus 410 is at the next corner to the right of the Stuartholme steps. This walk can also be combined with Walk No. 24 by walking a kilometre to the left along Sir Samuel Griffith Drive to Simpson Falls Road.

Walk key

1. Main gate | 2. Information Kiosk | 3. Fragrant plants and herbs | 4. The restaurant and gift shop | 5. Lagoons | 6. Giant golden bamboo | 7. Temperate zone | 8. Demonstration garden | 9. Tropical dome | 10. Japanese Garden | 11. Freedom Wall | 12. Common Australian garden shrubs | 13. The Totems | 14. The lake | 15. Palm grove | 16. Bunya forest | 17. The lookout | 18. Exotic rainforest | 19. Australian rainforest

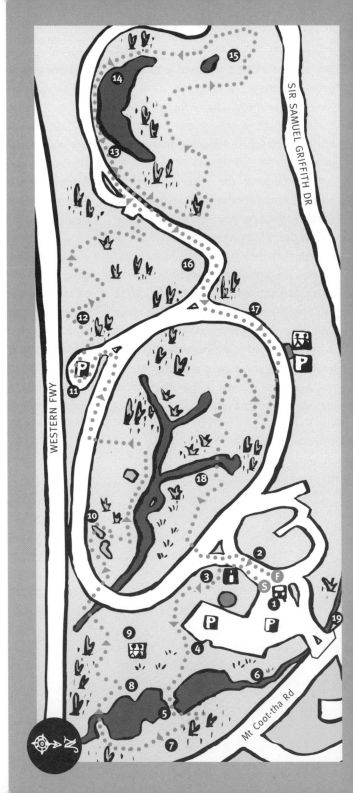

Walk No. 23

Mt Coot-tha Botanic Gardens
Bunyas and bromeliads

Start/Finish

The bus stop inside the gardens. Catch City Bus 471 from the corner of Adelaide and Albert Streets. These run hourly every day 10.10am–4.10pm.

Length/Time

4 km/1.3 hours
For a shorter walk, pick up brochures detailing the self-guided interpretative walks at the visitor's centre. The White Arrow Trail takes in the major areas only, and the Aboriginal Plant Trail identifies plants traditionally used by the Murri people.

Access

Although there are some quite steep grades, most of the main pathways are wheelchair-accessible. The Brisbane Mobility Map, available from City Council offices, gives details of all gradients. The gardens have a special section featuring scented plants for people who are vision-impaired.

Brisbane's second Botanic Gardens were begun in 1971 and officially opened in 1976, to complement the city gardens established 120 years earlier. They are situated in an ideal location at the foot of Mt Coot-tha, only fifteen minutes by bus from the city, and cover fifty-two hectares of land with more than twenty thousand plants from all over the world. This walk gives an overview of the extent and variety of the gardens, and includes visits to the Tropical Dome and the Planetarium.

The bus stops inside the **main gate** |1|, and the entrance is through the **Information Kiosk** |2|, a little way up the hill behind the bus shelter. This is where you pick up your Visitor's Guide.

Once through the kiosk turn left and follow the signs to the **fragrant plants and herbs** |3| area. This section was established especially for the sight-impaired, but it is a good test for the sighted as well, so shut your eyes and see how many plants you can identify. The plants smell strongest just after a rain shower.

The lagoons

Keep walking to the left until you get to **the restaurant and gift shop** |4|, temptations you should resolutely avoid at this point, walking instead down to the two adjoining **lagoons** |5| at the bottom of a slight slope. This area is sometimes used for outdoor theatrical performances, *A Midsummer Night's Dream* being a particular success. The grove of **giant golden bamboo** |6| on the left of the lagoons was planted last century when this was still a bushland park. Walk to the other side of the lagoons through this bamboo grove, or use the little bridge and feed the ducks on the way.

Continue clockwise through the plants of the **temperate zone** |7|. This part of the gardens is at its best in the cooler months, when azaleas, camellias and flowering bulbs are in bloom.

Cross the lagoon again at the far end, where the pink water lilies are as big as dinner plates. If you are interested in grasses and crop plants, detour right into the **demonstration garden** |8|.

Otherwise stay on the main path, where the fruit trees on the left are strictly for observation only, as they are sprayed heavily with insecticide.

The strange building you will see on the right is the **tropical dome** |9| where warm climate plants flourish in the controlled heat and humidity. The collection of exotic palms, vines and orchids give a whole new meaning to the term 'hothouse beauty', and the pond adds to the feeling of being deep in a flourishing tropical jungle.

Return to the path near the fruit trees and continue past the parking area on the left until you see signs for the **Japanese Garden** |10|, a gift from the Japanese government in gratitude for Brisbane's World Expo '88. This is a quiet place to rest for a while to absorb the tranquillity that this traditional minimalist style always seems to convey, with its subtly placed rocks, ponds and rippling water.

The Freedom Wall

Leave the Japanese Garden from the top right-hand corner. Walk left uphill across the grass to join the ring road. This is the most testing part of the walk.

On the way, notice the attractive conifer garden to the right, displaying plant specimens from many parts of the world, and also the bandstand, strategically placed to allow graded seating on the grassy slope in front of it. Follow along the steep incline of this road until you come to the commemmorative **Freedom Wall |11|**, built to mark the fiftieth anniversary of the First World War. The names of Australians who died during that war are commemorated in individual bronze plaques, which have an interesting history.

Originally the War Graves Commission supplied blank brass plaques to individual families who could engrave them in any way they liked. But some of these were so badly done, and so many were being constantly polished, that the names often wore out, so all plaques have been replaced by new bronze ones, uniformly lettered.

As you leave the Freedom Wall, go past the carpark and take the path to the left going downhill through the **common Australian garden shrubs |12|** on the right. Further to the right, on the cooler southern slope below the ring road, bunya pines have been planted.

The area you are crossing now is still under development – it is designated as a cool temperate rainforest site – so make your way uphill again to join the ring road. Turn left and continue down the hill where, if you walk across the grass from the next car park, you can get a closer view of **the Totems |13|**, just near the lake. This impressive sculpture by West Australian Lyn Moore consists of a number of poles ranging in height from 1.5 metres to 6 metres, in ironbark so tough it had to be cut with a chain saw. This sculpture was originally commissioned for the Brisbane Expo '88, and was later donated to the Mt Coot-tha gardens.

Opening Times

The gardens: daily 8am–5.30pm (September–March), and 8am–5pm (April–August).
The Tropical Dome: daily 9.30am–4.30pm.
The Sir Thomas Brisbane Planetarium: Cosmic Skydome show lasts 45 minutes Wed–Sun (3403 2578). Free guided tours Mon–Sat at 11am and 1pm, except public holidays. Ring 3403 2533 for further information, or ask at the Information Kiosk.

Refreshments

The Planetarium Gardens Restaurant is open 9am–5pm, and there are a number of drinking fountains throughout the gardens.

Route Notes

Collect a free Visitor's Guide at the Information Kiosk, which has a map of the entire area showing a web of tracks, more than can be detailed in this walk. You will probably get slightly lost, but as long as you follow the general directions suggested in this book, you will cover the main areas and end safely back at the bus stop. Toilets (including disabled toilets) are located at the entrance, the restaurant and the tropical dome.

The lakes

Wander clockwise around the edge of **the lake |14|**. This part of the gardens is not visited as often as the sections closer to the entrance, so it is amazingly peaceful and undisturbed. Passing through rainforest and landscaped streams, it is difficult to believe that the Western Freeway is only a few hundred metres away. Leave the big lake and walk towards the bridge at the foot of a much smaller lake, which will take you to the **palm grove |15|**, planted only in 1991 but thriving in the subtropical climate.

From here, use the map to circle round the lake, either past heathland and melaleuca wetland at the lower level, or through the acacia and eucalypt forest higher up. Above you on the left, but fortunately hidden from view behind the ridge, is the huge Mt Coot-tha quarry, which has provided rock for Brisbane's roads since 1919 and is likely to operate for many years to come. When it is finally closed, the site will be incorporated into the Botanic Gardens.

Return to the ring road now, taking any path you like, turn left and follow the road above the **bunya forest |16|**. The bunya pine is an indigenous Australian tree, producing cones full of nuts which were highly prized by the Murri people, who celebrated the ripening of the nuts as a time of festival, trekking long distances through the bush to gather them and perform ceremonial dances.

The pines are still young, and although they seem widely spaced at the moment, they grow so tall and wide that in a few

Tropical dome, Mt Coot-tha

years time they will form a veritable forest. Other plants native to the Bunya Mountains are being planted here as well, so that the area will reflect one of Queensland's most important natural habitats. There is currently discussion going on as to whether this area should be fenced off, to protect visitors from the heavy nuts which fall as the pines develop.

Continue on the ring road until you come to **the lookout |17|** on the left. Stop here – you will be glad of the drinking fountain by now – and take in the magnificent views of Brisbane framed by the gardens below.

Leaving the lookout walk past the toilet block on the left to the ring road, and look back to see a brilliant display of bougainvillea. From the ring road take the path to the right and wind your way down to the **exotic rainforest** |18|. This area offers many alternative paths along pretty waterways, and the Visitor's Guide will help you find your way back to the ring road and the Information Kiosk.

Australian rainforest

Either take the bus back to the city, or spend another half-hour exploring the **Australian rainforest** |19| on the left-hand side of the road leading to the main gate.

This area is covered by the official Aboriginal Plant Trail guide, available from the Information Kiosk. This brochure not only points out plants like native ginger, cluster figs, spear trees and cabbage palms, but explains how they were used by the original inhabitants of the area for medicine, shelter, food, hunting and carrying equipment. This trail goes around the oldest part of the gardens, planted in 1974. Even without a brochure, the different plants can be identified from the useful interpretive signs placed beside the path.

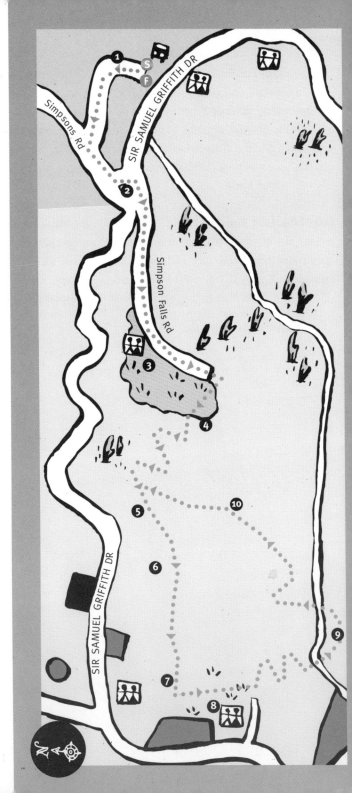

Walk key

1. Carwoola Street | 2. Traffic island | 3. Peter's Pound picnic area | 4. Sign to Simpson Falls, Eugenia Circuit, Brush Box and Grey Gum | 5. Simpson Falls | 6. Main track | 7. Brush Box track | 8. Grey Gum track | 9. Fire access road | 10. Black wattle forest

Walk No. 24

Simpson Falls
& the Eugenia Circuit
Bush trekking

Start/Finish

Carwoola Street, Bardon. Stop
22 is the terminus of City Bus
375 from Adelaide Street.

Length/Time

6.5 km/2.5 hours

Tips

Stout boots or good walking
shoes, sunscreen and a hat,
insect repellent and a drink
and perhaps a snack, as there
are no shops or kiosks along
the way. The picnic area is very
attractive, so you may want to
make a day of it by taking
lunch with you.

Access

The track ranges from
well graded to rough and
quite steep. It is not suitable
for wheelchairs.

In 1880 a large part of Mt Coot-tha was
set aside as a reserve. Today this area
of untouched bushland provides an
extensive recreation area only five
kilometres from the centre of the city.

Its main waterway is Ithaca Creek,
which eventually becomes Breakfast
Creek and flows into the Brisbane River
at Newstead. This walk goes through
Peter's Pound picnic area (named
democratically after one of the
gardeners who worked on it),
and follows West Ithaca Creek up to
Simpson Falls (Captain Henry George
Simpson was head of a pioneer family
who once owned a dairy farm at the
bottom of Mt Coot-tha). It continues
anticlockwise to complete the Eugenia
Circuit. This walk can be combined with
the other Mt Coot-tha walk (Walk 22).

Walk the few metres back from the bus terminus at **Carwoola Street** |1| to Simpsons Road (the main road), and turn left. At the **traffic island** |2|, 250 metres ahead, take the road signed Simpson Falls, a paved road which follows the creek upstream. About 750 metres on the right is **Peter's Pound picnic area** |3|, well equipped with a children's play area, barbecues supplied with fuel, a shelter shed, toilets and water taps.

Greedy wildlife

Lazy over-fed goannas are often to be seen around this spot picking up picnic scraps, and kookaburras always welcome scraps of meat — one of life's minor joys is to watch a kookaburra kill a raw sausage by dropping it from a tree, as if it were one of the snakes which are their natural bush food. By contrast the bush turkeys, grown over-familiar with human beings over the years, can be more of a nuisance than a delight. Cut through the picnic grounds in an upstream direction until you come to **a sign** |4| saying 'Simpson Falls, Eugenia Circuit, Brush Box and Grey Gum', the last two referring to other picnic areas in the park.

The track now follows the creek upstream through dry rainforest, a cool sheltered region where ferns and reed-like native grasses grow along the creek bed.

As the track zigzags higher up the side of the valley, the rainforest is replaced by open eucalypt forest, with tall elegant gums towering above the undergrowth of flowering native shrubs.

West Ithaca Creek

After about 15 minutes you will reach **Simpson Falls** |5|, where the stream flows over a wide rock ledge into a pretty rock pool ten metres below. Like all local water courses it is seen to best advantage after the seasonal rains in the summer, but it is never so turbulent that it cannot be crossed, even after a February downpour.

Spend a little time relaxing at the falls, and then return to the **main track** |6| and follow the signposts marking the Eugenia Circuit. As you leave the creek bed behind, the track soon starts to climb again, and you will be grateful for the wooden bench at the top, where you can regain your breath while admiring the view of the boulder-strewn course of another creek which cuts its way through a deep wooded gully. On the slope across and above the creek, black wattles grow in profusion, giving off their honey-sweet perfume during the spring flowering season of August and September. They are lovely to look at and to smell, but their pollen may be distressing to people susceptible to hay fever and asthma, who should take care during these months. In late summer, after they have shed their bark, the tall straight trunks of the eucalypts take on subtle shades of grey, beige, rust, ochre and creamy tan, a landscape painter's delight.

Along the creek again

The track now follows this second creek for part of its course, crossing and recrossing it several times. After twenty minutes or so you will come to a sign on the right pointing to **Brush Box** |7|. Do not take this track but keep going on the circuit track for another five minutes, until on the right you see the track to the **Grey Gum picnic area** |8|.

Cooling down on the ridge

Once you have passed this point the circuit track becomes rougher and steeper, but at the top, cool breezes channel up from the numerous gullies to the ridge, and there is always the comforting thought that from here on it is downhill all the way. So slog along until you reach the **fire access road** |9|, turn left and, half a kilometre along, pick up the rough track again on the left, at the signpost for the Eugenia Circuit.

Opening Times
The park is never closed.

Refreshments
Only a water tap at Peter's Pound.

Route Notes
There are toilets at Peter's Pound. From here it is essentially a bush walk, with many rocks and tree roots to be negotiated, so inexperienced walkers should take care. Bikes are not allowed.

Don't be tempted to follow the fire access road – it may look inviting, but it makes a precipitous descent further on, navigable by 4WD vehicles but not recommended for human legs.

The track now narrows and follows a ridge through thick **black wattle forest** |10|, with small boulders littering the area. As the track descends towards the Simpson Falls again, these boulders actually form the path, so the going is rough and should be negotiated with extreme care.

Once back at the falls, cross over to the starting point and retrace your steps to Peter's Pound, from where it is only a few hundred metres to the bus stop.

Walk key

1. Nudgee Beach |
2. Modern houses |
3. Sea wall | 4. Tabbil-ban
Dhagun track | 5. Bird-hide |
6. Nudgee Beach Store

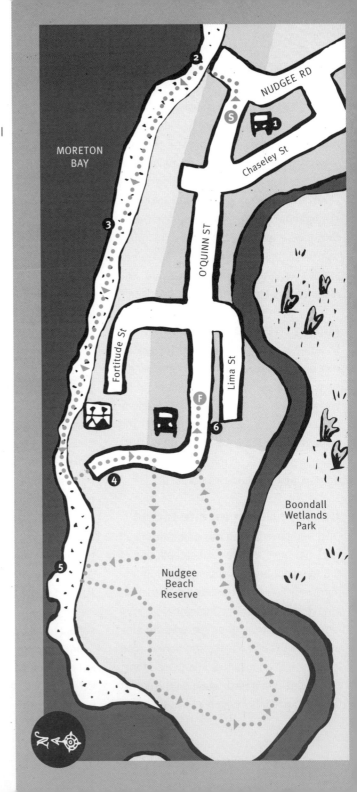

Boondall Wetlands
Bird life on the bay

Start

Southern end of Nudgee Beach – City Bus 306 from the Adelaide and Edward Street corner to O'Quinn Street, Nudgee. Ring Transinfo on 13 12 30 for timetable details.

Finish

O'Quinn Street, Nudgee Beach – City Bus 306.

Length/Time

3 km/1 hour

Tips

A large part of this walk is through unsheltered spaces, so take appropriate precautions, including insect repellent and a bottle of water.

Access

The boardwalks are quite level, and are wheelchair accessible for 1.5 kilometres. The beach may require some clever footwork when the tide is high, but it is quite safe.

Located only 15 kilometres from the city, these are Brisbane's largest remaining wetlands. In 1990 the site was declared a protected reserve, so that today the tidal flats, mangroves, salt marshes and freshwater wetlands provide a vital and undisturbed habitat for bird, fish, animal and plant life, as well as being an important recreational area.

From early October to late March the wetlands are home to exotic wading birds from Siberia, China, Alaska, Mongolia and Japan, while the winter months are the best time to see the local birds. This walk includes the serene foreshore of Nudgee Beach on Moreton Bay, then goes through part of the reserve via the Tabbil-ban Dhagun mangrove boardwalk. The route is accessible at all times, although the view many vary according to the tidal level. The local Murri word 'Nudgee' means 'black duck'.

Get off the bus at stop 38 in O'Quinn Street. **Nudgee Beach |1|** is a tiny settlement, consisting of a handful of houses and four streets, bordered by Kedron Brook to the south and Nudgee Creek one kilometre to the north.

Time seems to have stood still here; this is how many of Brisbane's small coastal settlements must have looked in the earliest days. But unlike many of the early settlers, today's residents are active participants with the Brisbane City Council in conserving the fragile wetland habitat in which they live.

From the bus stop, walk back a little way to Nudgee Road and take a left-hand turn to the waterfront. On the left are a couple of surprisingly **modern town houses |2|** on long narrow blocks facing the bay and catching all the breezes. Walk along the beach in front of these houses, or in the vegetated area if it is high tide, until you come to a path that cuts in a little way ahead and leads to a **sea wall |3|** fronting onto parkland.

The mud flats

Follow the sea wall for about a kilometre. At high tide the mud flats will be under water, but when they are exposed at low tide you will get an excellent view of the hundreds of tiny crabs that scuttle among the spreading roots of the mangroves. But remember the golden rule for behaviour in the reserve – look but do not touch.

Even at high tide, don't take this part of the walk too fast; rather take time to stop

Boardwalk and Bird-hide

and stare, for many of the treasures of the mud flats are slow to reveal themselves.

A little further along on the right, notices on the seawall explain how Moreton Bay has been identified as a wetland of international importance by the Ramson Convention of 1971, and set out the history of the development of the bay.

At the end of the seawall, cross the carpark diagonally to reach the **Tabbil-ban Dhagun track |4|**, which follows the edge of the bay and later the south bank of Nudgee Creek. The boardwalk begins here, and a few metres along, a 200-metre detour leads to a **bird-hide |5|**, from which exotic wading birds can be seen in an undisturbed environment. Local species such as the white-faced heron are common, while migratory birds like the bar-tailed godwit are around from early October to late March. Identification of the various species is made easier by the wall posters inside the hide. The hide also offers views of the Redcliffe peninsula and the Shorncliffe headland, and it is a good place to rest on a hot day.

Return to the main boardwalk, which wanders through mangrove flats with their abundance of bird life. At low tide, keep an eye out for crabs scuttling into their mud holes, especially the variety with one red nipper much larger than the other.

There are information boards at various points along the way, as well as plenty of seats that allow you to appreciate the serenity of this unique landscape at your leisure. At the end of the boardwalk, pass the cycle track on your left and continue back to O'Quinn Street. Opposite the bus stop is the **Nudgee Beach Store** |6|, an ideal place to have a coffee while you wait for the bus back to the city.

Opening Times

The wetlands are open every day of the year 6am–7pm.
The Nudgee Beach Store in O'Quinn Street closes at 5.30pm Mon–Fri, and 5pm Sat–Sun.

Refreshments

There are water taps in the picnic area, but the only drinks and snacks available are at the local convenience store in O'Quinn Street at the end of the walk.

Route Notes

The beginning of the walk is easiest at low tide, and the mudflats show fauna not visible at high tide. Tide times are given on the weather pages of *The Courier-Mail*, Brisbane's metropolitan daily newspaper. As this is a nature reserve, dogs are not welcome. Please do not remove shellfish from the area, disturb plant or animal life, or leave litter. There are toilets in the Nudgee Creek boardwalk area.

Walk key

1. Wynnum Station |
2. Wynnum Hotel |
3. Concrete bridge |
4. Moreton Bay | 5. Fish markets | 6. Shire Clerk's cottage | 7. Waterloo Bay Hotel | 8. Mt Carmel Convent | 9. School of Arts | 10. Wynnum Ambulance Station |
11. Manly Boat Harbour |
12. Cambridge Parade |
13. Royal Esplanade |
14. Stone retaining wall |
15. Manly Railway Station |
16. Lota House |
17. Swimming pool |
18. Pandanus Beach |
19. Wynnum Central Railway Station

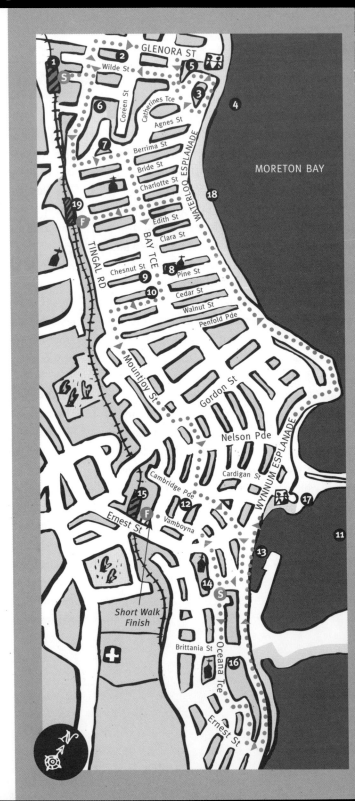

Wynnum–Manly
Oysters and islands

Start

Wynnum Railway Station.

Finish

Manly Railway Station or,
for the longer walk, either
a bus from Pandanus Beach
or a train from Wynnum Central
Railway Station.

Length/Time

7.5 km/2.3 hours
10–11 km/3–4 hours.
The area is so attractive it
is worth scheduling a full day
and breaking for lunch near
the Manly Boat Harbour,
or taking the half-day trip
to St Helena Island.

Tips

Make sure you are in
good condition, as there
are plenty of hills.

Access

The walk is on made
roads with no rough tracks,
but it contains some very
steep stretches. The steep hills
make it difficult, but not
impossible for wheelchair users.

These attractive bayside suburbs were first settled in the 1860s when the area was known as Oyster Point, although development did not really take off until the coming of the railway line in 1889. They have now become dormitory suburbs of Brisbane, but they retain their friendly small-town atmosphere, and are particularly attractive on days when Brisbane itself is sweltering in the heat.

Leave the train at **Wynnum Station** |1| and walk up Thorne Street, turning left into Tingal Road as far as the roundabout. Turn right into Glenora Street where, on the right, you will come to the **Wynnum Hotel |2|**, successfully hiding its 1870 origin behind built-in verandahs and an art deco exterior. This is the favourite pub of workers on the fishing fleet moored in Wynnum Creek. Turn right into Fox Street, crossing over a **concrete bridge |3|** which was erected in 1921, replacing the shaky wooden 19th century structure. Fox Street becomes Cusack Parade at this point, so from here turn left into Agnes Street and then left into Waterloo Street, where it's worth stopping to take in the features of **Moreton Bay |4|**.

A pattern of islands

The two closest islands are Green Island to the south and St Helena, the old convict gaol, to the north. Over on the southern horizon you can see North Stradbroke Island. To the north is the mainland peninsula of Redcliffe, and on a clear day you see Moreton Island far off much further north.

Walk north along The Esplanade, where some old cottages still remain – Nos. 43 and 39 in particular have attractive iron lace verandahs. At Wynnum Creek the **fish markets |5|** can be seen on the opposite bank, much reduced from the glory days of the 1930s when they employed 108 people and landed 2000 tonnes of fish annually.

Follow the creek to the left and cross Fox Street Bridge again. Turn left into Wilde Street and then left into Tingal Road where, a little way ahead on the left past a huge Moreton Bay fig tree, is the pretty little **Shire Clerk's cottage |6|**, built in 1890 and sensitively restored in 1984.

Turn left at the roundabout into Berrima Street. Here the dual personalities of the **Waterloo Bay Hotel |7|** present a contrast between the old and the new – the original section with the open verandahs was built in 1889, while the public bar was opened thirty years later.

Colonial buildings

Turn right into Bay Terrace, where the Wynnum shopping centre has a pleasing small-town feeling, and there are some good buildings at the southern end – the old post office on the right, now a medical centre; the two extremes of the Christian spectrum, the Baptist (1912 onwards) and the 1905 Roman Catholic Guardian Angel's churches, on the left; the exquisite **Mt Carmel Convent |8|** (1915) across the road, with deep verandahs designed to give the nuns in their heavy habits some relief from the heat; and, on the corner, that great Australian institution the **School of Arts |9|**, originally built in 1915 as a citizens' library, with extensions added later to satisfy the local residents' desire for horticultural shows, country balls and weekly dances.

Turn right here into Cedar Street, where you pass the old **Wynnum Ambulance Station |10|** on the corner of Tingal Road, a fine example of civic pride and responsibility, as the local community paid half the cost of its erection in 1926. There are some attractive old houses in this street, too.

Turn left into Tingal Road and up the hill to where it becomes Mountjoy Terrace, turning left after three blocks into Gordon Parade, which gives a fine view of the bay, with the **Manly Boat Harbour |11|** ahead and Wellington Point in the near distance.

Turn right into Carlton Terrace, cross Nelson Parade and turn left into **Cambridge Parade |12|**, where the rows of old shops still have street awnings supported by posts in the footpath, a sensible custom in the subtropics but one which heartless modern town planners, who probably never get out of their cars except in air-conditioned shopping centres, have deemed to be unnecessary and untidy. Some of the older style shops were built with top-floor flats, and feature unusual verandahs which project right over the footpath.

You have now walked more than six kilometres and are probably ready for a rest, and Cambridge Parade is the ideal place to stop for a drink or a snack.

Wander down to **Royal Esplanade |13|** after this, which runs along the side of the bay, and spend some time enjoying the vista of hundreds of yachts moored in the boat harbour.

Royal Esplanade

Go south along the Esplanade (with the water on your left), and notice some attractive houses and flats on the right behind lush greenery. At Falcon Street, just past the Wynnum Manly Yacht Club but before

Opening Times

Cat-o-Nine-Tails ferry trip to St Helena Island leaves from the William Gunn jetty, behind the Manly Swimming Pool, at 11am on Saturday, Sunday and school holidays, and around 9.15am weekdays. The half-day trip includes a guided tour by actors in period costume, and an optional lunch ($8 extra). Bookings are essential (3396 3994).

Refreshments

Numerous shops and cafés along the route.

Route Notes

The Brisbane City Council Heritage Trail brochure (Series 8, Wynnum–Manly), available at Brisbane City Council Service Centres or 69 Ann Street in the city (3403 8888), gives fuller information about the history of individual buildings for those who are interested. Get a copy before you catch the train from Brisbane. Toilets at various places along the beachfront.

the Royal Queensland Yacht Squadron, turn right and go up the hill, noting the huge **stone retaining wall |14|** that was built in 1933 to supply relief work for the unemployed during the Great Depression. You may be able to see small concrete heads of Australian animals (and some human ones as well) between the stones, put there by creative workmen in the same way as medieval stonemasons amused themselves by carving gargoyles and misericords while they were building the great cathedrals of Europe.

At this point, you must decide whether 7.5 kilometres is enough, or whether you want to commit yourself to the longer walk of 10–11 kilometres. For the longer walk, turn left into Oceana Terrace.

For the shorter walk, turn right into Oceana Terrace, where at the intersection with Kooralgin Street there is a fine view of Moreton Bay (named by James Cook in 1770 when he sailed on the outside of the islands, thinking they were part of the mainland). On the left you can see the Port of Brisbane, Moreton Island, St Helena Island, Green Island and Stradbroke Island. Follow Oceana Terrace, then turn left into Yamboyna Street and follow it to the **Manly Railway Station |15|**, where you can catch a train back to Brisbane.

Views of the bay

For the longer walk, follow Oceana Terrace across Valetta and Britannia Streets and notice **Lota House |16|**, the oldest building in the area, which began life as a retire-

Manly Boat Harbour

ment home for a rich grazier, and now offers the same wonderful views to a group of less affluent old men, who know it as the Edwin Tooth Memorial Home for the Aged.

Make your way back to The Esplanade by turning left into Grace Street, right into Armytage, left into Ernest and then left again into The Esplanade. Going north, with the bay on your right, walk back past the boat harbour, which was built in 1958.

The **swimming pool |17|**, filled at high tide with sea water which is kept in by valves along the sea wall, was another civic project from the depression years. Close to this you will find the ferry which makes daily boat trips to the ruins of the prison settlement on St Helena Island (see Opening Times for full details of this trip).

Continue up The Esplanade around Darling Point to **Pandanus Beach |18|**, which only came into being this century, when the stone sea wall built during the depression allowed the salt flats to be reclaimed as parkland. In the local Murri language the word Winnam (spelt by white settlers as Wynnum) means Place of the Pandanus Tree. Buses to the city leave from here, or else you can turn left into Florence Street for the one-kilometre walk back to **Wynnum Central Railway Station |19|** (not to be confused with Wynnum Railway Station, where you got off the train).

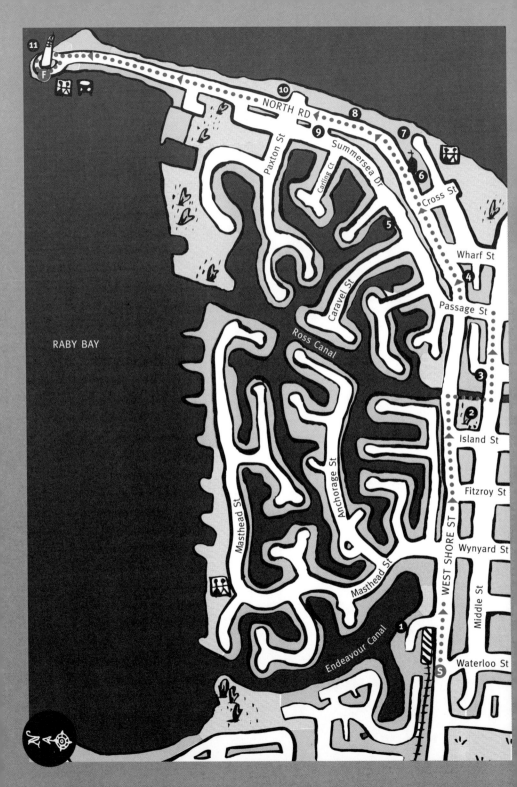

Cleveland

Capital potential

Start

Cleveland Railway Station –
an hour by train from Roma
Street or Central Station.
Phone 131230 for timetables.

Finish

Outside Lighthouse
Restaurant – return to Brisbane
by National Bus route 5 or 5X.
(Information 3245 3333)

Length/Time

4 km/1.5 hours.

Tips & Access

No major hills here,
although some of the paths
are unsuitable for wheelchairs.
Take a hat.

Part of the Redlands Shire, and therefore outside the Greater Brisbane area, Cleveland Point is a good 37 kilometres from the CBD by fast train. It was here that George Gipps, governor of NSW, landed in 1842 to ascertain its suitability as a port. He was 'much pleased with the appearance of Cleveland Point', but as he waded through the mudflats, the black ooze ascended to his knees and quite ruined his top boots. This sealed the fate of Emu Point – it lost its chance of becoming the colony's open sea port. But Cleveland developed as a separate settlement, and by the 1880s fashionable people were coming down from Brisbane to catch the sea air.

Walk key

1. Cleveland Railway Station | 2. Ross Creek | 3. No. 200 Middle Street | 4. Cleveland War Memorial | 5. Raby Bay | 6. Anglican church | 7. Grand View Hotel | 8. Cassim's Cleveland Hotel | 9. Poinciana trees | 10. The old courthouse | 11. Cleveland Point

Leave the train at **Cleveland Railway Station |1|**. Turn sharp left and follow Shore Street West, which is not clearly signed, but is the main road, with Raby Bay on the left. This side of the street is not shaded, so it is better to cross over and walk past the older houses on the right. Go past the Cleveland Bowling Club and take the path which goes off to the right, along the bank of **Ross Creek |2|**. Follow this to Middle Street, which runs parallel to Shore Street West.

Turn left here, and almost immediately on the left is **No. 200 Middle Street |3|**, a Victorian cottage which was the doctor's residence in the early days of settlement, and used for medical purposes until the 1930s. It is now the administrative headquarters of the RSL.

Almost immediately behind it, set a little way back from the road, is the station master's house, built in 1889 when the railway to Cleveland Central was first opened for traffic, thus making a day trip to Cleveland much easier for Brisbane residents. These days the building has a new life as solicitors' offices.

Turn left into Passage Street, where across the road is the old police station, a public building in the standard turn-of-the-century Queensland style. At the roundabout, veer right into Shore Street North, where the **Cleveland War Memorial |4|** commemorates local residents who served in the First World War. The names of those who served their country in later wars are also recorded here.

On the other side of the road the extensive new development of **Raby Bay |5|** begins in earnest, sweeping right around the bay almost to the end of the point. Many people consider this canal estate a blot on the landscape, but you may like to detour for a few minutes and wander past the kind of luxury houses that are seen in lifestyle magazines.

There has been a great deal of concern from environmentalists about the loss of the mangrove swamps, which had to be drained before building could begin. This procedure, they argue, disturbed the food chain and therefore upset the delicate ecological balance of the area.

Just past Cross Street is the tiny **Anglican church |6|**, built in 1873. In those days it was the spiritual home of the gentry, but today it is more popular for fashionable weddings, and if you take this walk on a Saturday afternoon you are sure to see at least one bridal party with entourage.

Queensland's oldest pub

Everything is old around this area – by Australian standards, that is. Past the church is an old banyan tree reputed to be the oldest in the state, and the next building is the **Grand View Hotel |7|**, Queensland's oldest pub. The original building dates back to 1851, although much of the present building was added in the 1870s. It has been in continuous use as a hotel since it was built, and when Queensland separated from NSW in 1860, the Grand View was used as the polling station.

Like all old buildings, of course, it has a ghost – the barmaid is prepared to swear blind that she saw a mysterious stranger in the bar after closing time, who disappeared when she confronted him, while the barman has been known to tell visitors that he sometimes feels an inexplicable breeze when all the doors are locked. But as he also admits that he's a notorious liar, there's an immediate problem – should you believe a liar who says that he tells lies?

In recent years the pub has undergone a very happy restoration – here the standard old heritage colours of slurry green and mustard yellow harmonise with the surroundings, and the old iron lace verandahs are in superb condition. Even the additions, like the three bandstands in the Emu Point bar and the lych gate leading out towards the bay, seem very much at home. It was at this spot, incidentally, that Governor Gipps made his ill-fated landing.

The Grand View really is a beautiful hotel both inside and out, surrounded by poincianas, frangipani and banyan trees. Even if you're not stopping for a drink, wander inside to see the photographs of old Queensland in the Heritage Hall, and also pick up some tourist information brochures for even more information about the area.

Half a block further along, **Cassim's Cleveland Hotel |8|**, a heritage property, has just been restored after being subdivided into flats since 1929, when it was heavily damaged during a storm. John Cassim was the first publican in the district. He managed the Grand View for

Opening Times

Grand View Hotel – bar and pokies, lunch and dinner Mon–Sun, 8am–late. Lighthouse Restaurant café bar, lunch and dinner Mon–Sun, 10am–midnight.

Refreshments

The traditional place to stop for a drink and lunch is the Grand View Hotel, which dates from 1851.

Route Notes

Unless you intend to spend a full day in the area, plan the trip very carefully to co-ordinate public transport to and from Cleveland. Get timetables for the return bus or train journey before you leave. There are public toilets in the reserve at the end of the Point, and in G. J. Walter Park behind the church.

Francis Bigge until 1860, when he built this hotel for himself.

Along the point

Just past Cassim's, a roundabout marks the beginning of a short avenue of spreading **poinciana trees |9|**, probably brought from Asia Minor by an early trade commissioner, John Finucane, who introduced many exotic trees to Cleveland Point. Turn right into Paxton Street, where **the old courthouse |10|** and lock-up is now a restaurant – a plaque on the wall gives a brief history of the site.

The old jetty, the departure point for boats to Stradbroke Island, used to be at the end of Paxton Street, but now only a few old wooden piles remain beyond the mangroves. But there are still excellent views, to the popular holiday destination of Stradbroke Island and, between it and the mainland, notorious Peel Island, which was used as a leper colony until 1949.

Return to Shore Street North and continue along the poinciana avenue where, on the left and the right, are some very pretty old cottages. Nos. 151, 153 and 159 are good examples of the early period of Cleveland's development, and on the left you will see a cottage with a rusty galvanised iron roof. A little further along on the left is a tiny heritage cottage, one of the few left from the time when the lighthouse keeper, the policeman, shopkeepers and postmen all lived here.

Next comes an unsheltered stretch of road running along the side of the bay. The

Grand View Hotel

mangroves which once lined the shores have all disappeared, but seagulls and ibis can be seen scavenging in the mudflats at low tide. The road ends at **Cleveland Point |11|**, with a small picnic shed and toilet facilities close to the old lighthouse. This now functions as a restaurant, its original duties having been taken over by a modern navigation beacon further along.

The point offers good views of the bay islands. North Stradbroke and Peel Islands are on the right and then, going anticlockwise, Moreton Island with its huge sandhills, Mud Island and, at the mouth of the river, St Helena Island, which used to be a prison. The huge cranes are on Fisherman Islands, now the site of the Brisbane Container Terminal. To the left is Wellington Point, at the end of Raby Bay or a drink. The Lighthouse Restaurant, next to the reserve, is a good place to stop for lunch. Here you can sit outside catching the cool bay breezes and hearing the water lapping against the sea wall and, at low tide, watch gulls and herons as they fossick for food in the lush mudflats which so disturbed Governor Gipps.

On cold days, move inside where it is snug, reminiscent of an old English pub, where there's always a roaring fire going, and the horse brasses on the exposed timber beams seem half a world away from the sub-tropics. Conveniently, the bus for the return trip to Brisbane stops immediately outside the restaurant.

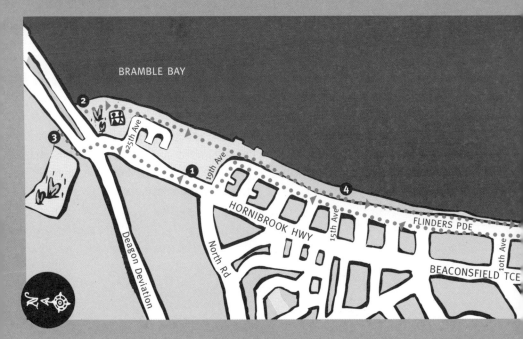

Walk key

1. Eventide Home | 2. Decker Park | 3. Hornibrook Highway viaduct | 4. The waterfront | 5. Sandgate Railway Station | 6. Town Hall | 7. Sandgate Pier | 8. Moora Park | 9. Cabbage Tree Head | 10. Baxter's Jetty | 11. Queensland Cruising Yacht Club | 12. Sandgate Golf Club | 13. Fisherman's Co-op | 14. Shorncliffe Railway Station | 15. Morven

Start

Walk A: Sandgate Railway Station, then Redcliffe bus to southern end of the Hornibrook Viaduct.
Walk B: Sandgate Railway Station

Finish

Walk A: Sandgate Railway Station
Walk B: Shorncliffe Railway Station

Length/Time

Walk A: 4.5 km/1.5 hours
Walk B: 5.5 km/about 2 hours

Tips & Access

Sandshoes or sneakers are a good idea, for you may be tempted to go rock-hopping or take a walk along the sand. There are some steps and a few steep hills in Walk B, but Walk A, along the sea front, is completely flat.

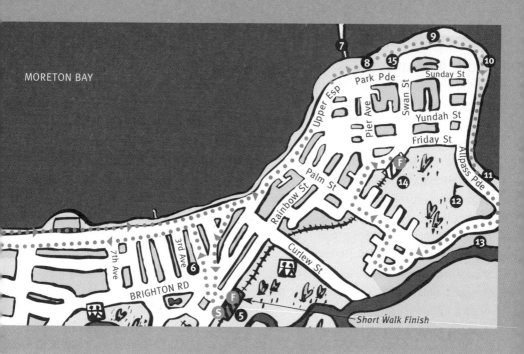

MORETON BAY

Park Pde
Upper Esp
Pier Ave
Swan St
Sunday St
Yundah St
Friday St
Allpass Pde
Palm St
Rainbow St
7th Ave
3rd Ave
BRIGHTON RD
Curlew St
Short Walk Finish

Shorncliffe & Sandgate
Escape to the bay

Suggest to any Shorncliffe resident that their suburb is really part of
Sandgate and you're liable to be in big trouble. The Shorncliffe area, the
original civic centre of what is now called Sandgate, still clings proudly to
its separate identity. Strangely enough, until recently Shorncliffe was merely
a locality name, which came from a map of 1873 describing the 'shorn cliff'
of the coastline at this point. This walk treats both suburbs with equal
respect, for when you have forested wetlands, bayside walks, beautiful old
buildings and birds like egrets, herons, lapwings and kingfishers, the actual
name of the locality hardly matters.

Walk A: Waterfront walk

At Sandgate Railway Station catch the bus to Redcliffe, No. 20, 21 or 30, leaving approximately half-hourly at 5 minutes to and 25 minutes past the hour. Ask the driver to let you off at the **Eventide Home |1|** about 3 kilometres along.

Continue north along Beaconsfield Parade/Hornibrook Highway past **Decker Park |2|** on your right. Cross at the lights at the entrance to the **Hornibrook Highway viaduct |3|**, where there are excellent views of the calm waters of the Pine River and the distant D'Aguilar ranges. This is pelican country, and they can sometimes be seen perching on top of the streetlights.

At the start of the viaduct take the steps to the left and follow the path across to and under the Houghton Highway – but mind your head. Then follow the path all along **the waterfront |4|** south towards Sandgate. It skirts Decker Park and the Eventide Aged People's Home, linking up with Flinders Parade, where there is a bikeway and a safe grassy verge for pedestrian traffic.

Measure your progress along Flinders Parade by the cross streets, numbered from Twenty-fifth to First Avenue. Among all kinds of fascinating old houses, look out for a two-storey blue art deco house behind old palm trees between Twelfth and Thirteenth Avenues; Cremorne, at No. 154, built in the early 1900s for John McCallum the theatrical entrepreneur; Meridian at No. 130 Flinders Parade, from the late 1880s; Torquay at No. 50; and Rothsay at No. 21. It is said that some of the old houses on

Flinders Parade were built from timber washed down the river from the great flood that devastated the CBD in 1893.

To finish the walk, turn right into Cliff Street at the end of Flinders Parade, follow the roundabout to Bowser Street, and catch the train from **Sandgate Railway Station |5|**. To continue the walk, cross to the pathway at the end of Flinders Parade and follow the directions for Walk B.

Walk B: Headland walk

As you leave **Sandgate Railway Station |5|**, Bowser Parade is straight ahead, with the lovely old post office on the left, and the **Town Hall |6|**, built in 1911, on the right. The lovingly landscaped area is a fine example of civic pride and cultural sensitivity.

Flinders Parade, Sandgate

Cross Brighton Avenue and go down Second Avenue to Flinders Parade, turn right and go south along the foreshore. One might wonder why perfectly good street names like Petty, Wilson, Cooksley, Jane, Henry and Tully were changed in the early 1900s into the monumentally boring First, Second, Third Avenues etc. Perhaps the early civic fathers thought the citizens of Sandgate/Shorncliffe could count better than they could read.

If the first scent of sea air turns your mind to fish and chips, you will not find better on the bay than at Doug's Café at 60 Flinders Parade. Flinders Parade was named after Captain Matthew Flinders, who does not really deserve such an honour, because he sailed on the inshore side of the bay islands without even noticing the mouth of the Brisbane River on his circumnavigation of the continent between 1801 and 1803.

Walk along Flinders Parade until it ends, and then either take the path along the foreshore or the steps to the upper level. Both routes trace the outline of the peninsula – you get more sweeping views from the higher level, but you are closer to the sea on the lower path.

The first part of this section looks out onto Bramble Bay. Around the headland, the **Sandgate Pier** |7| juts out below **Moora Park** |8|. A Mr Nehemiah Bartley complained in the 1860s that Sandgate had 'no piers, no German bands, no circulating libraries, no bathing machines and no society', but we hope he hung around until 1882 when the pier was built. For one shilling and sixpence return on the ferryboat *Olivine*, the Humpybong Steamship Company would ferry commuters from Shorncliffe (the proper name for the suburb at this point) to Woody Point from where – often green around the gills after the choppy trip – they would catch the train into the city and then return late in the afternoon to do the whole thing again. They were the pioneering days, when stamina, as well as a strong stomach, was called for. The foreshore walk here along **Cabbage Tree Head** |9| is shaded by wild cotton trees, figs and casuarinas, but the cabbage trees have mostly disappeared.

Opening Times

Sandgate Golf Course may be used by non-members Mon, Wed, Fri at any time, or Sat, Sun after 3pm. Green fees apply.

Refreshments

On the shoreline is the **Café on the Park,** a quaint little building which sells local crafts like tulle fairy dolls, dried flower arrangements and Dr Chan's skin cancer cures as well as hamburgers. This is where Shorncliffe gathers on Sunday mornings, where a special breakfast is offered while you watch the pelicans and gulls on the mudflats through the trees of Moora Park.

Another option is to take fish and chips from Shelley Inn to the beach at Baxter's Jetty, with its view of the Yacht Club.

On Sinbad Street, on the banks of Cabbage Tree Creek, is the **Fisherman's Co-op** where the fish is always freshly caught and cooked.

Route Notes

There are public toilets in Moora Park, Flinders Parade and the Sandgate foreshores.

The stretch from the Baptist church in Cliff Street to Allpass Parade has been famous for a hundred years as Lovers Walk, and it is well enough lit for people to walk there in confidence even at night.

In Moora Park, just past the pier, the band rotunda is no longer in use, but it is a lovely spot for a picnic, and a perfect place for children to bounce on the highly sprung wombat and turtle rockers, or swing their cares away in old tractor tyres.

The seafront

All of the charm, and what there is of the action, of Shorncliffe is on the seafront. From **Baxter's Jetty |10|** to Cabbage Tree Creek it is boaties' territory, with the **Queensland Cruising Yacht Club |11|**, an Air Sea Rescue base, and the T. S. Paluma Sail Training Centre for naval reserve cadets cheek-by-jowl along Allpass Parade.

Here too you'll find the prawn trawlers moored, sadly reduced from their original strength of a 130-plus fleet, but adding some rugged reality to the scene. Prawns and sand crabs are still the main catch, although 90 per cent goes south to the restaurants of Sydney and Melbourne. The rest of the fish is bought by other co-ops up the coast.

Up on the headland is the **Sandgate Golf Club |12|**, established in 1921. The links, currently being redeveloped, are built on salt pans and mud flats, which makes them ideal for those who like a flat course that's not too taxing. The only obstacles you're likely to find are the terns and sacred ibis

Moora Park

who tend to graze on the greens. The greens are open to the public (see Opening Hours), and the fees are very moderate .

Allpass Parade eventually becomes Sinbad Street, which continues along the banks of Cabbage Tree Creek, and is where you'll find the **Fisherman's Co-op |13|**. Turn right into Palm Avenue and almost immediately left into Wharf Street, where No. 20 is a house with an interesting rotunda.

To get to **Shorncliffe Railway Station |14|**, the end of the line, turn right into Ashford Street, left again into Palm Avenue, cross the railway line, turn right into Kate Street and then right into Railway Parade.

Heritage houses

A more interesting walk back to the station is to go back to Allpass Street past the golf course and take Yundah Street off to the left. It is lined with fig trees and full of very old houses in various states of repair. Naracoopa at No. 99 was built in 1897 and has an interesting 'Widow's Walk'. Turn right at the top into Signal Row and right into Park Parade to see Haddington at No. 34, built in 1876; Berwick on Tweed, which used to be Mango Cottage, at No. 32 (built

1872); Shorncliffe Lodge (No. 16); and **Morven** |15|, originally called Cressbrook and built in 1864. It was used for US Army billets during the Second World War, and is now St Patrick's Boys' College.

At the end of Park Parade turn right into Swan Street and right again into Railway Parade which, as you might expect, leads to Shorncliffe Railway Station |14|.

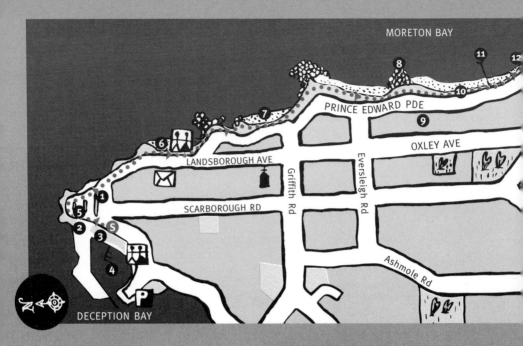

MORETON BAY

PRINCE EDWARD PDE

OXLEY AVE

LANDSBOROUGH AVE

Griffith Rd

Eversleigh Rd

SCARBOROUGH RD

Ashmole Rd

DECEPTION BAY

Walk key

1. Fifth Avenue | 2. Reef Point Esplanade |
3. Thurecht Park | 4. Scarborough Boat
Harbour | 5. Reef Point Beach |
6. Scarborough Beach | 7. Queens Beach
North | 8. Rocky point | 9. Weeping figs |
10. Captain Cook Park | 11. The Jetty |
12. First Settlement Memorial Wall |
13. Shops along Redcliffe Parade |
14. Redcliffe Point | 15. John Oxley Memorial |
16. Suttons Beach | 17. Seventh Day Adventist
Church | 18. Redcliffe Cemetery | 19. Roll
Out the Barrel Cooperage | 20. Wreck of
the *Gayundah* | 21. Woody Point | 22. Palace
Hotel | 23. Express Bus | 24. Pelican Park |
25. The old viaduct | 26. Houghton Highway

Start

City Express Bus from Edward
and Queen Streets (outside MacArthur
Chambers) Mon–Fri. Alight at the
Scarborough terminus. At the weekend
take the train to Sandgate Railway
Station then Blue Route Bus 20/21.

Finish

Buses back to the city run along
Scarborough Road/Victoria Street and
Landsborough Avenue/Oxley Avenue.

Length/Time

Redcliffe Jetty 4 km/1.25 hours
Scotts Point 7 km/2.5 hours
Pelican Park 9 km/3 hours

Tips & Access

Take a hat and sunscreen.
Excellent wheelchair access.

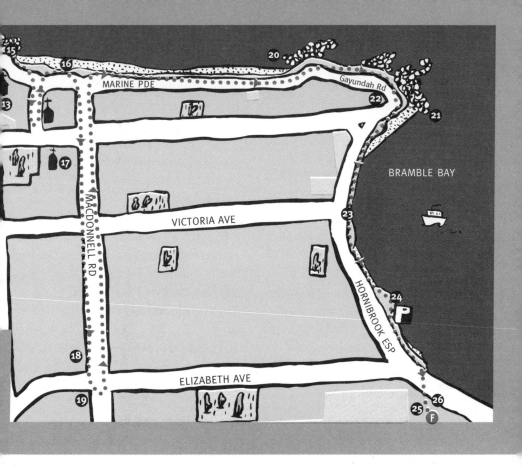

MARINE PDE

Gayundah Rd

BRAMBLE BAY

MACDONNELL RD

VICTORIA AVE

HORNIBROOK ESP

P

ELIZABETH AVE

Walk No. 29

Redcliffe Peninsula
I do like to be beside the seaside

Long before white settlers came to the area, the Redcliffe peninsula was occupied by a Murri clan called the Ningi Ningi. The first white person to land there was Matthew Flinders, who named the area Red Cliff Point in 1799; he was followed by John Oxley in 1823. The Ningi Ningi were not hostile to white people, but a party of convicts and their guards set up camp at Humpybong Creek in 1824, free settlers arrived in the 1860s, and the Ningi Ningi were soon driven away.

This walk begins at the northern end of the peninsula, and follows the coast of Moreton Bay south from Scarborough to Pelican Park, offering easy beach walks, excellent views and an historical overview of the area.

From City Express Bus 540, continue walking up Scarborough Road until you come to **Fifth Avenue |1|**, where you turn left. From Blue Route Bus 20/21, get off at Fifth Avenue and turn left, towards the boat harbour and fishing fleet (clearly signed). The friendly shop at the camping ground in **Reef Point Esplanade |2|** can give you information about the area (see Opening Times).

Bird O'Passage Parade

At the junction of Fifth Avenue, Reef Point Esplanade and Thurecht Parade turn into Bird O'Passage Parade on the other side of **Thurecht Park |3|**, which leads to the **Scarborough Boat Harbour |4|** where hundreds of boats are always moored. The views across Deception Bay to the Glasshouse Mountains are stunning. Thurecht Park has the biggest spreading cotton tree you are ever likely to see, just perfect for climbing.

Wander back along the Esplanade until it reaches the **Reef Point Beach |5|**, just past Second Avenue. From here, take the cycle path and boardwalk which follows the coastline south, sometimes hugging it closely, sometimes going inland for a few metres.

There is good fishing along this stretch of coast, but for swimming try **Scarborough Beach |6|**, which has a toilet block, or **Queens Beach North |7|**, five blocks

further south. The rocky outcrops of the many little points and headlands are good for exploring, too, and the beach facilities are beautifully maintained.

If you prefer to keep to the road, which changes its name many times, just follow the brown Tourist Route signs, which will save you getting lost and take you past the most interesting houses and streetscapes.

If you're walking along the beach, leave it at the **rocky point |8|** between Queens Beach and Queens Beach South. Find Shields Street, and from it take the first street on the left, which is not signposted but is in fact Prince Edward Parade. This leads under a thick avenue of shady **weeping figs |9|**, and four blocks later crosses Klingner Road.

Captain Cook's mistake

Turn left here to explore **Captain Cook Park |10|**, named after the famous explorer who came close to land when he named Morton Bay, which was how he spelt it on his charts. This led to one of his rare navigational errors, for he assumed that Moreton and Stradbroke Islands were part of the mainland. The memorial is a great lump of rock that contains a piece of stone from Whitby Abbey, in the English town from which Cook set sail.

The impressive Norfolk pines that grow all along the foreshore here are native to Norfolk Island, not to the peninsula, but they have taken well to life on the mainland and become a feature of the area. Redcliffe is home to many important historical monuments, including **the Jetty |11|**, which is undergoing a major transformation. Before the Hornibrook Highway was built in 1935, providing access to the peninsula by car, the two previous jetties on this site played an important role in landing people and provisions coming from Brisbane by ship. The new jetty will have a halfway house to provide shelter, and at the end there will be a restaurant and a kiosk.

The development of the entire foreshore on the peninsula is a model of sensitive restoration. The old bathing pavilion is now truly wonderful in its full art deco glory, and well-kept boardwalks lead down to picnic shelters on the beach.

Further south is a double curved **First Settlement Memorial Wall |12|**, unique in that it not only records the names of the white settlers, but commemorates the original inhabitants of the Ningi Ningi clan of the Undabi tribe, who had been here for at least 2000 years before white settlement.

The **shops along Redcliffe Parade |13|** may look like the usual commercial mix, but many of the buildings behind the modern glass shop fronts go back a long way. The Pier Picture Theatre opposite the jetty now has shops at street level, but the present building dates from 1947, while the three-storey Cominos Arcade (1942) was Redcliffe's first high-rise building.

The Ambassador Hotel is now painted a rather alarming shade of green, probably to commemorate Patrick O'Leary, who in 1881 built it on the site of the 1824 convict barracks.

Opening Times

Shop at Scarborough camping ground: open daily 7.30am–5.30pm
Roll Out the Barrel Cooperage: Mon–Fri 8.30am–4.30pm, Sat 8.30am–11.30am

Refreshments

If you begin the walk at lunchtime, Morgan's seafood café and restaurant, a Queensland institution, offers fish fresh off the boat in venues ranging from takeaway through casual dining to 5-star luxury.

Route Notes

A full-colour brochure, showing the Redcliffe Heritage Trail in full detail, is available free at the Redcliffe City Council offices (just past the RSL near Anzac Parade), and at other tourist outlets.

If you are exhausted after these four kilometres, you can pick up the local bus back to Sandgate in Redcliffe Parade opposite the Commonwealth Bank.

Ironstone cliffs

No visit to Redcliffe would be complete without a stroll over the reef at **Redcliffe Point |14|**, composed not of limestone but of ironstone, and easily accessible at low tide. There is spectacular bird life here at dawn and sunset, and the cliffs themselves show how the area got its name.

Just north of this reef, at the mouth of a little watercourse called Humpybong Creek, a small group of soldiers and their prisoners landed on 13 September 1824 to form a convict settlement. The huts they left behind when they returned to Brisbane Town were called 'dead huts', or humpybong, by the local Murri people.

On the headland overlooking the reef is the **John Oxley Memorial** |15|, which is remarkable for having many of its historical details incorrect. But it affords superb views down the beach to Scotts Point and South Reef, and across Moreton Bay as far as Fisherman Islands at the mouth of the Brisbane River far to the south.

The southern beaches

The next beach to the south is **Suttons Beach** |16|, where the mullet fishing is reputed to be even better than the excellent amenities on the beach front. Here in Pavilion Park are elegant shelters offering protection from the sun, a gracious bathing pavilion and a dignified toilet block. You have a choice of walking along the cycle path which skirts the sandy swimming beach, or on Marine Parade high above it. If you are interested in unusual church architecture, turn to the right into Sydney Street from Marine Parade and walk about 250 metres to the corner of John Street, where the **Seventh Day Adventist church** |17| makes a unique statement.

First Settlement Memorial Wall

Those with a particular interest in early history as documented in headstones may like to detour inland here to visit the **Redcliffe Cemetery** |18|. Turn right from Marine Parade, as the beach road is now called, into MacDonnell Road, where a rather dull 2.5 kilometre walk of twelve blocks will reward you with gravestones going back to 1884.

The cemetery is one of the few in Queensland that has headstones for Murri people – at least seven are buried here, and there is an affectionate memorial to Boama, or Sammy Bell, 'the last of his tribe', erected by his friends from Woody Point in 1913.

While you're in this area, it is worth going a little further to visit Noel Sullivan's **Roll Out the Barrel Cooperage** |19| at 299

MacDonnell Road just over Snook Road, which is the second on the left past the cemetery (see Opening Hours). This is one of the few cooperages in Australia still making oak kegs, wooden beer kegs, and wooden vessels of all kinds.

This may be a good time to catch the bus back to the city as the walk, once you return to Suttons Beach, is pretty much more of the same. The bus runs along Victoria Avenue, the second major street on the right off MacDonnell Road.

For serious walkers, though, it is an easy walk down the cycle path, and down at Scotts Point is the **wreck of the** *Gayundah* |20|, built in 1885 and used as a warship until after the First World War, when she was retired to the ignominious role of a sand and gravel barge, and was eventually towed down here to be beached in 1958.

Woody Point |21| is next, with a pretty jetty and a fine safe swimming beach. The **Palace Hotel** |22| here has an unrivalled view from the upstairs lounge and it offers a very peaceful place to stop for a while.

You have now reached the southern point of the peninsula, and the main road on the right is the Hornibrook Esplanade. The **Express Bus** |23| route back to the city joins this road at the intersection with Victoria Avenue, and you can either pick it up here, or keep walking down through Apex Park to Bells Beach, another quiet sheltered swimming area.

Just past Bells Beach are the landscaped grounds of **Pelican Park** |24|, where the pelicans are fed every day at 10am.

The Hornibrook Highway

This is the best place to catch the Express Bus back to the city, because Clontarf Beach, the final stretch of coastline, is really rather dull.

As you leave the peninsula in the bus, notice the pylons on **the old viaduct** |25|, the Hornibrook Highway, which are reminiscent of those on the Indooroopilly Bridge back in Brisbane. The Hornibrook Highway was built in 1935 of ironbark logs, and at 2.78 kilometres it is the longest viaduct in Australia. It used to be a toll bridge, but was closed in 1979 when the new **Houghton Highway** |26| was opened. Today it is used by the local people for fishing, romantic strolls at sunset, and for good views across the bay and the inlet.

The City Express Bus 540 (Mon–Fri only) goes back to Edward Street in the city, while the Blue Route bus 20/21 goes to Sandgate Railway Station for the train journey to Central Station.

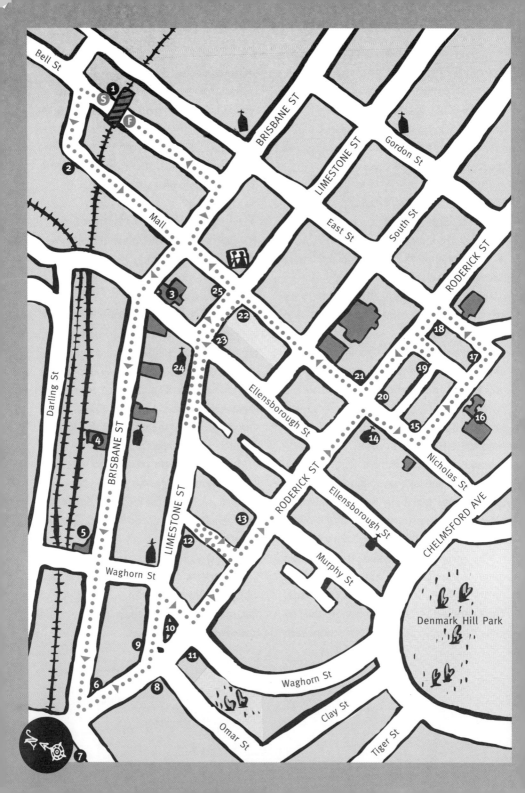

Ipswich

Heritage and history

Start/Finish

Ipswich Railway Station

Length/Time

4 km/1.3 hours

Tips

Ipswich is generally three or four degrees hotter than Brisbane in the summer and correspondingly colder in the winter, so dress appropriately.

Access

Most places are wheelchair accessible, but there are some very steep hills.

Even though it is now practically a suburb of Brisbane, Ipswich was one of the earliest Queensland towns, and once rivalled Brisbane as a centre of commerce. Its fortunes were built on coal and agricultural products, and it has managed to retain more of its historical buildings than Brisbane has.

This walk concentrates mostly on those buildings, some of which date from the 1870s when the town was established.

Walk key

1. Ipswich Railway Station | 2. Ipswich City Square | 3. St Paul's Anglican Church | 4. Flour Mill | 5. Metropole Hotel | 6. Federal Hotel | 7. City View | 8. No. 2 Burnett Street | 9. Brick cottage | 10. Baines Park | 11. Ozanam House | 12. Iron-roofed house | 13. Carrington Guest House | 14. Lutheran Church | 15. The Chestnuts | 16. A. E. Wilcox School of Nursing | 17. Police Station | 18. Court House | 19. Ginn Cottage | 20. Chermside and Mayorene | 21. Masonic Temple | 22. Green square | 23. Ipswich Technical College | 24. Ipswich City Uniting Church | 25. Sculpture

Leaving **Ipswich Railway Station** |1|, cross Bell Street diagonally to the right into Union Place. On the right is Murphy's Town Pub, an attractive hotel now functioning as a coffee shop and bar.

Turn left and walk across the shopping mall into **Ipswich City Square** |2|, a pleasantly landscaped area with young shade trees and plenty of seating. From the Square turn right into Brisbane Street, the oldest in Ipswich. Cross to the clearly marked Information Centre on the other side and pick up booklets about the Top of Town heritage trail.

Top of the Town

You are now going towards the commercial area west of the city centre, known for more than a hundred years as the Top of Town, which is being redeveloped and revitalised as part of a government and council project. On the left is **St Paul's Anglican Church** |3|, the oldest Anglican church in Queensland. Built in 1859, it has good stained-glass windows, hammer-beam ceiling trusses and many memorials to Ipswich citizens, including a chapel dedicated to the memory of Mavis Parkinson, one of the Australian missionaries killed by Japanese soldiers in New Guinea in 1942. The pipe organ dates from 1860. Next door the splendid rectory, completed in 1895, has decorative timber trims and wide verandahs.

Cross over Ellenborough Street then look right down West Street for a fine view of St Mary's Roman Catholic Church (1904) and its grand presbytery (1876). Cross West Street to the Lifeline building to admire the pressed metal lining under the eaves of the verandah, a characteristic quite commonly found in this street. A little further along on the right is the old **Flour Mill** |4|, with its original brick exterior. Inside, the building has been transformed into a shopping arcade with a snack bar open on Sundays. You get the best view of this building from the opposite side of the street.

Continue along to the corner of Waghorn Street. On the right is the **Metropole Hotel** |5| (1900), now called the Harp of Erin. Like many buildings in the town it was designed by George Brockwell Gill, and shows his characteristic style of dark brickwork thrown into contrast by a lighter-colour render. The bullnosed verandah marks it as a pre-1914 building, and the steel columns and lace-work brackets are very fine. By now you have reached the peak of Brisbane Street, climbing steadily all the way, to be rewarded by a panoramic view of the Great Dividing Range. The lowest dip is Cunningham's Gap and on the right is the rounded outline of Mt Cordeaux.

Cross now into Burnett Street. The **Federal Hotel** |6|, which retains its classical parapet with Palladian motifs, and the **City View** |7| opposite, designed by the ubiquitous G. B. Gill, may tempt you to a different kind of reward.

The charms of Burnett Street

Refreshed or not, turn left into Burnett Street, where there is a fascinating mix of old houses, some dating back to the 1860s and earlier. No. 7 has recently been restored while its neighbour, Notnel (No. 8), was built in 1859, and is one of the few remaining houses with an attic and dormer windows. One of the motifs on the iron lace that adorns **No. 2 Burnett Street |8|** is that of the cornucopia, or horn of plenty, a fitting symbol for the town's rich agricultural associations. In 1875 the two-storey house at No. 1 replaced a timber cottage built by William Berry in 1848.

You are now at the corner of Limestone Street, named after the rock for which Ipswich is famous. The first people to quarry it were convicts sent up from Brisbane Town, and free settlers used the limestone, with its veins of chalcedony and fine-grained quartz, to make decorative walls and garden edgings.

Turn left down Limestone Street, noting Nos. 111 (now a restaurant), 109, 107 and 105, all altered since they were constructed in the 1880s, but still retaining some of their original charm. No. 103 is unusual for the concave curve of its verandah and the slate roof, the only complete roof of this kind in Ipswich. Cross the road to see No. 108, a small **brick cottage |9|** that from 1869 to 1876 was a boarding and day school. Retrace your steps until you reach Waghorn Street on the left, which borders **Baines Park |10|**. This is not as tranquil as it looks – in springtime nesting magpies often make vicious attacks on people walking through the park. A notice warns people 'Beware Magpies'.

Refreshments

There are coffee shops in the Ipswich City Square and the Flour Mill on Brisbane Street, and also a number of hotels along the route.

Route Notes

Ipswich, as the ticket collector at the railway station commented not so long ago, is closed on Sunday, so if you are planning a Sunday excursion, keep in mind that places to eat and drink will be limited. The advantage, though, is that there are relatively few people about.

Follow Waghorn Street to the left to the junction with Roderick Street and look uphill to the right for a view of **Ozanam House |11|**, built in the 1880s for a bootmaker. The diagonal timber bracing on the verandah is outstanding, and the glass panes in the French doors on the verandahs have unusual curved tops.

Turn left down Roderick Street to see a mix of architectural styles, ranging from colonial to postwar economy. No. 60 is built right to the edge of the footpath, a characteristic of very early houses in this area. Take a detour left into Murphy Lane, where there is a very old weatherboard **iron-roofed house |12|**, and a lush mixture of garden trees including mangoes, bananas, frangipani and various palms.

Come back to the Roderick Street corner to see, at No. 66, **Carrington Guest House** |13|, originally a hospital. It was built in 1906 in Federation style, with elaborate timber fretwork in the gables and window hoods. On the opposite corner is Brickstone with unusual dormer windows.

Behind these houses the streets rise steeply to a ridge timbered with palms, hoop pines and eucalypts, and dotted with more fine houses with commanding views.

Some very special houses

At the corner of Ellenborough Street, on the left, is a rare old house with its shop still attached. Across the road, No. 38 is also built right on the street and has a lovely terracotta chimneypot. Nos. 34 and 36 also have details worth discovering – the art nouveau archways at No. 34, and the bull-nosed verandah at No. 36.

Cross and turn right into Nicholas Street and walk up the hill with the **Lutheran Church** |14| on your right. Mona Lodge is on the corner of Meredith Lane and higher up, on the Court Street corner, is **The Chestnuts** |15|, a delightful little house with many decorative details and a cool garden full of overhanging trees.

Turn down Court Street past The Chestnuts. On the right the ugly outbuildings of the Ipswich Hospital make a stark contrast to the **A. E. Wilcox School of Nursing** |16|, next on the right. This is the oldest building in the hospital complex, and is

Timber fretwork sunhood

surrounded by large old trees including mangoes, jacarandas and Moreton Bay figs. The original iron lace on the front porch gives some idea of what an elegant building it must have been in 1887.

Turn left into East Street. On the corner is the red-brick edifice of the **Police Station** |17|, built during the Second World War and occupied initially by the US Military Police. A much more attractive building is the old **Court House** |18| on the next corner, completed in 1859, just in time for the declaration of Queensland as a separate colony from New South Wales. The Court House is now a community cultural centre.

A murky history

Turn left into Roderick Street and look back to see the ridge of Limestone Park outlined against the sky. A little way up Roderick Street make a detour into Ginn Street to see **Ginn Cottage |19|** (1859). Its present function as a restaurant hides a murky past – the original residents, William and Eliza Jane Ginn, lost their son to typhoid caused, so Ginn believed, by the unbearable stench from the earth toilets of the court house opposite.

Return to Roderick Street, noticing the stately mansions at 30 and 30A Roderick Street, **Chermside** built for Alfred Tully in 1890, **and Mayorene |20|** built for his son Alfred in the late 1920s. Turn right into Nicholas Street, where you pass the **Masonic Temple |21|**, built in 1928 in a style later known as Interwar Free Classical, a description which covers all kinds of architectural peculiarities, including Doric columns and Corinthian capitals on the fluted pilasters. Don't miss the pretty **green square |22|** on the corner of Limestone Street, which links the Soldiers' Memorial Hall in Nicholas Street to the **Ipswich Technical College |23|** in Limestone Street.

Turn left into Limestone Street and go past the college, another work from the drawing board of G. B. Gill. It is a very elaborate building, with a lantern or raised skylight in the roof, urns on the parapet, and different styles of arches on the first and ground floors, as advocated in the Free Classical design theory.

The best view of the college is to be had by looking back across Ellenborough Street. Continue up Limestone Street to Wilson Lane on the left-hand side, where there is a fine view of the grand houses on the ridge leading to Denmark Hill. Retrace your steps, past the **Ipswich City Uniting Church |24|** on the left. Built in 1858, this is the oldest church in Queensland in continuous use.

Once you have recrossed Ellenborough Street, continue along Limestone Street and take the next left into D'Arcy Doyle Place, named after the artist who grew up in Ipswich. At the end of D'Arcy Doyle Place is a charming **sculpture |25|** of children playing in a creek, another work by Rhyl Hinwood. Turn right into Brisbane Street, then first left into Bell Street to the Ipswich Railway Station.

Bibliography

Brisbane City Council *Heritage Trail Series*, numbers 1–11.

Fisher, Rod, *Petrie Terrace Brisbane, 1858–1988: its ups and downs*, Brisbane, Boolarong Press, 1988.

Fisher, Rod and Brian Crozier (eds), *The Queensland House: a roof over our heads*, Brisbane, Queensland Museum Publications, 1994.

Johnston, W Ross, *The Call of the Land: a history of Queensland to the present day*, Brisbane, Jacaranda Press, 1982.

O'Connor, Terry, *A Pictorial History of Queensland*, Brisbane, Robert Brown and Associates, 1996.

Scott, Bill, *Portrait of Brisbane*, Brisbane, Rigby, 1976.

Siemon, Rosamund, *The Mayne Inheritance*, Brisbane, UQP, 1998.

Index